Design Thinking in Schools

Design Thinking in Schools

A Leader's Guide to
Collaborating for Improvement

John B. Nash

Harvard Education Press
Cambridge, Massachusetts

Paperback ISBN 978-1-68253-419-9
Library Edition ISBN 978-1-68253-420-5

Library of Congress Cataloging-in-Publication data is on file.

Published by Harvard Education Press,
an imprint of the Harvard Education Publishing Group

Harvard Education Press
8 Story Street
Cambridge, MA 02138

Cover Design: Wilcox Design
Cover Image: Liyao Xie/Moment/Getty Images

The typefaces used in this book are Minion Pro and Myriad Pro.

CONTENTS

PREFACE

This book presents a process through which school leaders can address a myriad of organizational and educational challenges in their school, from the mundane to the relentlessly complex. The process, called human-centered design, or design thinking, can help create new solutions to problems schools face. This book describes the techniques school leaders can use to reframe challenges by *thinking like a designer* to create unique, effective solutions.

Although the application of design thinking in education is not new, this book was written specifically to provide an explicit step-by-step road map for school leaders—including superintendents, principals, and teacher-leaders—to effect sustainable, student-centered change. In my experience, other guidebooks about design thinking on the market have limited utility for busy school leaders, and this has been part of my motivation for writing this book. The biggest gap in the current materials available for educators is a collection of examples. I've noticed that one of the ways my students and professional development participants prefer to learn is through case studies and examples. Most resources available now offer more of a "how to" than a "why" or a "what happens when." While this information is valuable, it tends come off as more of a checklist than a narrative. An irony in all of this material is that, although uncovering and telling another person's story is a key aspect of a successful design thinking process, the current works out there don't do this effectively—they don't tell stories that help readers see themselves and inspire them to try new steps. In essence, they don't practice what they preach. Last, and perhaps most important, other materials available to educators don't provide an overarching focus on students as participants, or codesigners, as this book does.

School leaders are uniquely positioned to bring together the stakeholders needed to invent the solutions demanded by today's educational environment. As you will read, I believe anyone can be a designer, and the processes and tools described in this book were themselves designed to be accessible and low-cost.

I was first exposed to design thinking when I was a social research scientist at Stanford University, long before I applied it in a school setting. There I was mentored by colleagues associated with my lab, the Stanford Learning Lab, including Larry Leifer, Sheri Shepherd, Doug Wilde, Bernie Roth, and Rolf Faste. When I later took a faculty position at Iowa State University in 2009, I grasped the opportunity to fill a gap I saw: that design thinking, while reaching teachers, students, the corporate sector, and even the developing world, had not been framed as a tool for shaping schools as organizations. Since that time, I have been working with preK–12 educators, higher education groups, statewide agencies, community foundations, international schools, nonprofit organizations, and other groups that support education. I have introduced design thinking in a variety of settings and shown how to apply it as a tool to solve tough problems both large and small. For example, educators might wish to

- reimagine how spaces in schools can support student collaboration
- create a new, innovative school schedule for an urban high school
- improve course offerings for students
- introduce school policies and instructional practices that give students greater agency
- enrich the early learning programs in an entire state

The process, tools, and worksheets included in this book have been adapted or created with school leaders in mind. They have also been tested in the field, and my most popular process, which involves school leaders codesigning change with students (in some cases with kids as young as fourth and fifth graders), has been used with over seven hundred educators since 2011 in workshops across the United States. My protocols for deep dives within a single site have been tested in schools or districts and in my own upper-division undergraduate/graduate course on design thinking at the University of Kentucky. The experiences of educators I have worked with at the elementary, middle, and high school levels are also included in this book as a way of showing how design thinking has resulted in solutions that have made a difference in the lives of educators and students.

It's through these settings and channels that I have also learned what can thwart design thinking and how to predict challenges schools may face as they take on the process. These hurdles are different at any given step of the process and can differ from challenges faced by designers in other settings.

One of the pressing problems for educators is how to serve all students equitably. In this book, I describe how schools have used design thinking to include the voices of students across the economic spectrum in both rural and urban settings. Design thinking gives leaders a natural opportunity to elevate the voices of those students who have been disenfranchised or overlooked and to empower them in the process.

My hope is that this book will move the conversation around school reform in a positive direction by enabling school leaders to leverage the collective wisdom and expertise of those around them. To borrow a phrase from David Weinberger, "the smartest person in the room is the room itself."[1] What's been missing up to this point are tools and processes that school leaders can use to tap into the wisdom of the people around them every day—their coworkers, fellow educators, students, and community members. Human-centered design allows superintendents, principals, and teacher leaders to see beyond what's within arm's reach and instead invent new solutions to challenges that until now have felt intractable.

INTRODUCTION

This book comes at a time when teachers and school leaders realize that solving the challenges facing modern schools is less about making good decisions and more about facilitating collective, coordinated action on the part of teachers, students, parents, and community partners. The challenges schools face are multifaceted, have numerous potential solutions, and with almost no exceptions, impact people. Many might call them "wicked" problems.

It's fashionable these days to talk about problems as being wicked, but what does that mean? The term comes from Horst Rittel and Melvin Webber, professors at the University of California, Berkeley, who in the 1970s suggested that people in professions where social planning and governance is the chief endeavor (teachers and leaders in schools would be in this group) have been "misled somewhere along the line into assuming they could be applied scientists—that they could solve problems in the ways scientists can solve their sorts of problems."[1] The issue, as Rittel and Webber tell it, is that the problems scientists and engineers focus on tend to be "tame" or "benign." In other words, it's very clear when a problem they are working on has been solved. On the other hand, "wicked problems," ones that are tricky, thorny, or problematic, are not always clearly formulated, nor does one always know when they are solved (or if they're solved at all).[2] Name just about any school program or initiative that is working suboptimally and you will probably find that the path to improving it is stalled thanks to its wickedness. Do any of the following sound like tame problems to you: optimizing the day pattern for all students, getting all teachers on board with technology, devising a graduate profile for all students, crafting a schoolwide culture of personalized learning, and ensuring every child is fully included in all programs and services. These challenges are just the *normal* problems school teams try to solve, yet each is classically *wicked*.

The challenges teachers and school leaders face are often resistant to simple, straightforward, or top-down solutions. Design thinking offers a process to address those problems by engaging a wide range of stakeholders in the pursuit of solutions with concrete outcomes that can be measured, such as increasing student engagement, improving school liking, increasing graduation rates, and increasing family engagement. Design thinking has promise for creating improvements in schools that are innovative, novel, and pleasing, and that in the process transform the culture by increasing empathy, collaboration, and optimism. This book is meant to outline that process in a way that is accessible for school leaders.

WHAT IS DESIGN THINKING?

Design thinking is a critical tool for simplifying and humanizing wicked problems.[3] To best define it, we should pull it apart and discuss first the word, *design*. What do you think of when you see or hear the word *design*? Perhaps you think of professions, such as architectural design, interior design, fashion design, or graphic design. Perhaps you think of creativity, beauty, or aesthetics. Some people think of verbs like *plan*, *strategize*, or *scheme*. For our purposes, you can consider design as a process that "intends to offer a concrete solution to a complex problem that is socially ambiguous and neither easy nor certain to comprehend."[4]

It is also a term you may take on as a moniker. There is nothing wrong with calling yourself a designer. One of my goals in this book is to have you act in more *designerly* ways. Consider the fact that design touches all aspects of our world, and the role of designers is to impact the human experience.[5] This being the case, as an educator you are likely already a designer; you just haven't been using the title. There is little in your world that has not been designed by someone, from the furniture around you to the curriculum your students follow in schools.

From Design to Design Thinking

When people in education talk about design thinking, it's often conflated with notions of classical design. This happens in many industries.[6] Historically, some form of design has been a part of the culture of organizations (chiefly businesses) since the 1950s, with traditional design permeating the likes of big corporations such as General Motors and IBM, where it influenced corporate identity and product styling in the 1950s and 1960s.[7] Modern design firms, such as Frog and IDEO, emerged between 1970 and 1990, articulating a transition from traditional design to designing systems and services.[8] Whereas earlier notions of using design in organizations were about aesthetics, the new focus was on applying the principles of design to the way people lived and worked.[9] And while the roots of design thinking can be traced to work in fields such as interaction design, participatory design, and user-centered design—bolstered by Nobel Prize recipient Herbert Simon's declaration that design is not just the purview of engineers—it's in the 2000s when design thinking comes into its own as a way to harness the creative problem-solving skills of designers to tackle nonengineering problems.[10] The 2005 launch of the Hasso Plattner Institute of Design at Stanford, better known as the dSchool, is an example of this.[11] In the last five years, design thinking has become a mainstream approach, even a whole-business strategy, for companies like SAP, Procter & Gamble, and Capital One.[12]

Quality of Experience

A common denominator among organizations leveraging design thinking is the notion of *quality of experience*. The example I love to tell over and over is that of Zappos. When I have the opportunity to share this example in a presentation, I'll ask, "How many in the room have heard of Zappos.com?" If I'm in the States, many enthusiastic hands go up. I then ask, "What kind of store is Zappos?" From those whose hands went up a chorus comes back: "Shoes!" It's reasonable they say so. Zappos, at its inception, sold chiefly shoes (and it still does, in addition to other apparel). And then I ask, "What's so appealing about Zappos?" Someone invariably explains that Zappos ships everything to you for free, return shipping is also free, and you can take up to 365 days to return items. Even though the things people love about Zappos don't have to do with shoes (notice people don't respond with "The shoes are great!"), to most people, Zappos.com is still a shoe store. But ask Zappos what kind of store it is and you'll get a different answer. As Tony Hsieh, Zappos' CEO, puts it, it is a service company that happens to sell shoes. That's interesting, isn't it? The CEO of many people's favorite place to buy shoes doesn't think it's a shoe store. And to sell more shoes, Tony Hsieh doesn't focus on shoes.

I had a personal experience that drove home his point. I once bought a pair of snow boots from Zappos and broke a strap on one of them within one minute of taking them out of the box (it was my fault). I sheepishly called Zappos' customer service line to admit my brutishness, expecting to have to pay for a replacement pair. Not only did Zappos offer to overnight a new pair of replacement boots for free, and let me ship the owner-damaged goods back for free, but for the kindness of vandalizing my own new boots they would make me a member of their VIP club with free overnight shipping for life. "Would that be all right, Mr. Nash?" the customer rep asked (I accepted).

Now, let's take Zappos' philosophy and apply it to schools. Ask just about anyone what schools do and they'll tell you they exist to educate kids. But what if we thought of schools in another light? What if we thought of schools as service organizations that just happened to educate kids? Schooling is a service provided to the public that is experienced by students. That experience should be amazing.

Shifting Expectations

There is an increasing desire on the part of the public to engage in transactions that are not only efficient but also a good experience. Take, for instance, the simple ubiquitous commodity, the cup of coffee. Coffee sold at one's local Quik Mart gas station is delivered on the transactional, Weberian premise of efficiency—*get in, get out*. When you buy a cup of coffee at the gas station you are buying, well, a cup of coffee. Conversely, the same product sold at, say, Starbucks is predicated on the premise of a transformational experience: *come in, stay in.* When you buy a cup of coffee at Starbucks you are buying an experience.

Now, we can debate who has better coffee, Quik Mart or Starbucks; neither enterprise appears to be going out of business anytime soon. What is not up for much debate is how, thanks in part to what Starbucks has done for coffee, other segments of society are catching on to how experience matters.

It's no accident, for instance, that transformations in the humanizing of the health care industry have taken place in the wake of increased attention to how people experience health care. Consider the work of Doug Dietz, principal designer at GE Healthcare, an $18 billion division of one the largest corporations in the world. The MRI machines Doug and his team deploy help countless thousands through the images they create, and, as it turns out, scare the hell out of children who are subjected to them. As many as 80 percent of pediatric patients must be sedated before they are calm enough to remain still for an MRI machine to do its job.[13]

Doug couldn't stand this, so he and a team went into action. Did they redesign the MRI? No. They redesigned the experience.

The team observed the children and gained empathy for what they went through. They talked with families, nurses, and other specialists. And, without making changes to the technology, the team solved the problem. A pediatric patient entering the MRI room today is in the center of an adventure story in a colorful room, covered floor to ceiling with characters that craft a story. Even the machine operators were provided a script so they could take patients through the adventure. "The number of pediatric patients needing to be sedated was reduced dramatically. The hospital and GE also got a benefit from this, because less need for an anesthesiologist meant more patients could get scanned each day and patient satisfaction scores went up 90 percent."[14]

Let's take the story at GE Healthcare and bring it around to schools. Before Dietz's epiphany, being placed in an MRI machine, for children, was a scary experience for which they were told, in so many words, "Just suck it up." Before Dietz's work, hospitals would put pediatric patients at further risk, through sedation, to get them to comply with the procedure.

After all, why should it be pleasant? The procedure is being done in the name of helping the patient. Experts are overseeing the process. Experts who know best.

It's hard not to think of schooling when one thinks of the MRI story in this way. Education, like health care, is managed by experts. Students are, for the most part, expected to accept the experience they are provided and, in case they don't care for it, they should also "just suck it up."

ADOPTING A DESIGN ATTITUDE

The management of modern schooling has been the purview of experts. A cult of expertise has reigned over schooling, particularly with the increased professionalization of educational leaders, thanks in part to numerous graduate schools and the growth of educational leadership in the field. The results are a double-edged sword. The expertise and knowledge base are vastly expanded. The cadre of those in decision-making positions, however, is constricted. Not perhaps in terms of people, but in terms of thought. As Hess notes, "[T]hose who have spent their career immersed in the rhythms of any profession come to regard its policies, practices, culture and routines as givens."[15] As a result, there are too many educational leaders who come into their position having been told throughout their training there's only one solution to every problem. Leaders who fall into this camp possess, according to Boland and Collopy, a decision attitude.[16] Such leaders:

- believe there exists a finite set of alternative solutions to problems, mostly provided by outsiders (other schools, vendors, the literature)
- assume it is easy to come up with alternatives to consider, but difficult to choose among them
- assume that the alternative courses of action are ready at hand
- are lulled into the belief that a good set of options is already available, or at least readily obtainable
- are trapped in the role of passive decision maker, making the untenable assumption that the alternatives presented in advance include the best possible alternatives

Why would skilled leaders opt for a decision attitude? One reason is that, as Stanford professor James Adams so aptly noted, "Few people like problems."[17] It's because of this, he continues, that the "natural tendency in problem-solving is to pick the first solution that comes to mind and run with it. The disadvantage of this approach is that one may run either off a cliff or into a worse problem than one started with. A better strategy in solving problems is to select the most attractive path from many ideas, or concepts."[18]

Contrast this with leaders who Boland and Collopy describe as having a *design* attitude. These kinds of leaders:

- work with stakeholders to develop custom solutions that are not known at the start
- are concerned with finding the best answer possible, given the skills, time, and resources of the team
- develop alternatives for local conditions; thus decisions about which alternative to select become trivial
- take for granted that the initiative will require the invention of new alternatives
- know that their stakeholders are best suited to say what their needs are, and options are created based on those needs
- are active designers on a team of decision makers who help develop new alternatives that are usually better

One reason schools receive a pass on making K–12 education an amazing experience for students is that school attendance is compulsory. It's not like public schools have to compete against each other for "customers" by offering the best experience possible. However, it's easy to see why companies do so—the better the experience, the more likely someone will choose one company over another. (Which company do you think I check first when I need shoes?) Let's look at some of the research. By 2016, 89 percent of companies surveyed by the research group Gartner believed that customer experience would be their primary basis for competition, up from 36 percent in 2012. And research from the Temkin Group suggests that consumers are six times more likely to buy a product, twelve times more likely to recommend a company, and, perhaps most telling, five times more likely to forgive a mistake if they are having a positive emotional experience in or around a purchase.[19]

What does this mean for teachers and school leaders? If you want student buy-in—which for schools means engagement, interest, perseverance, intrinsic motivation, and so on—you need to be thinking about the design of experience and how it can infuse every student-facing function. Sure, you may not be a banker with a mission to sell financial services or credit cards. And you may not be the purveyor of a cafe, selling coffee or croissants. But you are an educator, and you're in the business of passing along knowledge, via an education, to students. And if that experience for students sucks, your likelihood for success tanks. That's just simple math: if I'm a student, and I hate school, I'm probably not learning to my potential.

DESIGN THINKING AND EFFECTIVE LEADERSHIP

The process outlined in this book is consistent with the theoretical foundations that have emerged in the last decades around organizational success brought about by egalitarian and transformational approaches to leadership. One such approach is distributed leadership. Distributed leadership "is not something 'done' by an individual 'to' others, or a set of individual actions through which people contribute to a group or organization . . . [it] is a group activity that works through and within relationships, rather than individual action."[20] Design thinking can be seen as an act of distributive leadership. School leaders who read this book and practice its processes will, in essence, adopt a form of distributive leadership, empowering others to help come up with solutions and make decisions.

Design thinking also fits in with theories about effective principals as transformational leaders. Hallinger describes the evolution over time of the principal as leader, moving from the 1960s, when principals were viewed as program managers, to the 1980s, when school leaders entered an era as instructional leaders, to the 1990s and beyond, when the views of stakeholders outside of traditional leadership circles were given greater credence in decision-making in order to achieve greater buy-in and reach challenging organizational goals.[21] This latter approach represented "a new role for principals (and teachers) in problem finding and problem solving—a role increasingly referred to as transformational leadership."[22] An assumption underlying this shift is that "those adults who are closest to students—staff members and parents—are in the best position to make wise judgements about changes that are needed in the educational programme of the school."[23]

School leaders who have a predisposition to think transformatively, but lack a methodology to act on their desires, might well consider design thinking as an approach because it is all about leveraging the input and judgment of the user (typically the student) to prioritize key challenges and uncover novel, effective solutions to those challenges. Jesse Bacon, principal at Simons Middle School in Kentucky, has used design thinking as a way to bring students in as codesigners of learning spaces; he sums up the importance of using design thinking this way: "The problem we have as educators is that when we have a problem in front of us we go try to find somebody that's doing something on that problem and we try to copy it and bring it back. And while that may work sometimes, it's not very innovative, and it often fails."[24] Design thinking lets leaders make the transition from the experiences students are having now and the experiences students could be having. It's a way to fully capture what students need, what your community needs, and to create real fixes—not just something that you ask your teachers or your staff to implement as a result of visiting some place.

HOW TO USE THIS BOOK

Change at schools is constant. Community and policy actors make reform efforts, publishers push products, and school leaders often latch onto the latest scheme that promises to address the challenges in front of them. I've written this book to shift the focus of dialogue from problem solving to solution seeking.

The core of this book is organized around what I call phases of the design cycle, typically consuming one academic year. They are the kickoff, need finding, synthesis, brainstorming, prototyping, and implementation. In doing so, I have drawn on the approach advocated by the Hasso

Plattner Institute of Design (Empathize, Define, Brainstorm, Prototype, Test) and adapted it to fit the school context. I start with kickoff, because every design cycle begins with framing a challenge and assembling a design team. Then comes need finding, the term I chose because it involves understanding the unmet needs of people in the schools. Yes, need finding includes being empathetic to others, but there are additional ways to uncover people's needs that don't involve empathy, which I'll describe. The need finding phase yields much data for a design team, and thus it needs to be synthesized so teams can better gain insights from it. Once team members have synthesized the results from the need finding work, they are prepared to brainstorm solutions for their challenge. Brainstorming in design thinking is purposeful (and fun). It sets the stage for teams to select from among their many options the best ones to prototype. Prototyping is where you get to make your ideas real; then in the implementation phase you get to test them out to see which to keep and which to improve. Each chapter includes tools and assessments for completing key steps in each phase. To illustrate how the phases build on each other, you can follow the case of Lori Mills, principal of Jackson Elementary, throughout the book as she tackles the large challenge of making her school more student-centered. Mills is a composite of several school leaders I have worked with to incorporate design thinking in their improvement efforts. However, I have also included the stories of real leaders to illustrate how they can use design thinking to create better learning experiences for their students and, in some instances, to radically shift the entire culture of the school.

How do teams go through the steps, and what's the time commitment for each of these steps? Well, that depends of course on the complexity of the challenge, the size and cohesiveness of the design team, when members join the team, and the time periods during which the team schedules its work. Let's assume for the moment that you are the one kicking everything off—you've read this book and you've decided to form a team. How long does it take in terms of meetings? (This is not counting the mindshare you'll devote in other parts of your day. I'll warn you: design thinking turns you into a noticer. Once you understand how to frame problems, see unmet needs, and consider new solutions you may never see any common situation the same way again. So, while you'll devote time to the work of a specific project, you'll also be thinking about that work all the time.) To answer this question, I've included a rough estimate of time for each step in each of the six design thinking phases in this guide.

Each chapter also includes a discussion of obstacles leaders are likely to face in each phase of the design cycle and ways that they can be more effective. In the final chapter, I discuss the positive changes that school leaders experience when they practice design thinking.

Last, I've included two appendices. The first is "40+ Ways to Get to Know Your Students." This book has an overarching focus on students as participants, or codesigners, in the school change process. In the chapters that follow, you'll see that by getting to know your students better through empathetic conversations, shadowing, and glimpses into their everyday lives through photo studies, you gain insight on how to improve their lives. I describe these three approaches (conversations, shadowing, and photo studies) in detail so you can carry them out in your school. And the ways in which you can get to know your students are not limited to those three methods. Over the last several years, through discussions with my design thinking students and with educators across the United States and the world, I've curated a list of ways you can further get to know your students. Use the list to inspire your thinking on easy ways the adults in your school can be more attuned to what the lives of your students are like.

The second appendix contains an example of an Empathetic Interview Exercise. As you'll soon learn, empathetic conversations are a workhorse in the stable of tools available to you in the design thinking process. In this appendix I provide frameworks and sample question guides to take you through the process of holding productive and lively empathetic conversations.

Now let's get started.

CHAPTER 1

KICKOFF

For two days at the end of a hectic school week, Jackson Elementary principal Lori Mills and some of her teacher leaders attended an offsite professional development event conducted by the state's flagship university. The theme of the professional development was deeper learning and student agency, and Lori and her team were introduced to the topic of design thinking. Something gnawed at Lori all weekend after the workshop and when she and fourth-grade teacher Samantha met in the hall the following Monday morning, Lori pulled her aside.

"We're doing a really good job at getting input from parents, and I think I do a good job of getting input from staff, but what are we doing with the children? After all, they are who we are here for."

"What are you thinking?" asked Samantha.

Lori didn't miss a beat. "Over the weekend it just hit me. We need to have our students involved in conversations with adults more than they have been. Sure, we've surveyed the staff on what the school should be attuned to, and our site-based decision-making committee is representative of different voices, but after attending the workshop last week I can see how hearing from our students in authentic ways could help us not just improve, but redesign what we do. I can't stop thinking about our own students and what stories they have about their experience here."

A day later, Samantha opened her email inbox to find a message from Principal Mills to all teachers and staff.

To: Jackson Elementary Faculty and Staff
From: Lori Mills
Subject line: Join a school innovation team

Dear Jackson Community,
I am seeking volunteers to join me on a school innovation team that will apply the tenets of design thinking to discover and then address challenges facing our students and school. By joining the team, you will have a chance to walk in the shoes of students to better understand how Jackson Elementary impacts their lives. From this improved understanding the team will design, prototype, and test new solutions to the challenges discovered. The work will take place over one semester.

Consider the following traits of the kind of team member who is ideal for the tasks ahead. If you feel these describe you well, please let me know.

- *You are open minded.*
- *You are not afraid to hear ideas very different from your own.*
- *You're able to work collaboratively within a team.*
- *You often wonder how a school policy or practice will make students' lives better.*
- *You like to test out your hunches to find out if they will work.*
- *You're okay with letting others see work that's not complete.*

I look forward to hearing from you.

Sincerely,
Lori

Design thinking is about making someone's life better. How you go about doing that has a great deal to do with what aspect of their life you elect to improve. That, in essence, determines what challenge you'll address. And that's all part of the kickoff phase, which includes choosing a design team, assessing the readiness of your school for the design thinking process, and, finally, creating your initial challenge.

It's fair to wonder whether a challenge should be in place before a design team is selected, or a design team should be assembled first so members can help determine the challenge. Others have weighed in on this. For instance, IDEO, in *The Field Guide to Human-Centered Design: Design Kit*, recommends framing a design challenge, creating a project plan, and then forming a team.[1] The Frog *Collective Action Toolkit* urges its users to devise a challenge to address by looking at long-range impact, defining the problem you want to solve, and then setting goals and a timeline.[2] In the *Design Thinking for Educators Toolkit*, there are instructions on how to define a challenge and create a project plan.[3] And *The Designing for Growth Field Book* recommends steps on how to identify an opportunity, scope your project, draft a brief, and plan the design work.[4]

I've tried and taught most of these approaches and recommend the following steps to kick off the design process in schools: consider one or more general challenge areas, find the right people for a design team, and draft one or more specific challenges.

In my experience, most leaders come to this process with a general challenge in mind, such as a desire for more innovative thinking among teachers and students, an interest in more authentic student input, or an aspiration to have more personalized learning. Every school is different. At Bryan Station High School, a large public school in Lexington, Kentucky, there was interest in somehow improving the school schedule. At Havergal College, an independent K–12 girls' school in Toronto, Canada, educators wanted to address excessive smartphone use by students, and at Fairdale Elementary School in Louisville, Kentucky, staff wanted to explore what would surface if student voice were taken more seriously. In each of these cases there was ongoing conversation on each of the respective topics that was evident to leadership and staff. At some point a teacher leader or administrator at the school elected to talk to others about creating a design team.

CHOOSE A DESIGN TEAM

People who are new to design thinking sometimes confuse the work of a design team with that of a school committee. Committees tend to be charged with carrying out recurring needs within a school and giving advice or recommendations on policy or events. Curriculum committees or awards committees are examples. Design teams behave more like a project team whose mission is to accomplish a task by following a process. Thinking on your own, and in talking with others, create a list of three to five people you would invite to be on a design team. Teams don't have to be big to be inclusive. Yes, be as pluralistic as you can (see below). But don't make the team artificially big to satisfy a perceived need to include multiple voices. Design teams consist of a small group of people who, as a part of their work, will actively seek the voices and input of others. So a core of four to six people is adequate. In forming the team, consider the following things: What do you sense will be the nature of the general challenge you hope to solve? Is there a clear technical capability or certain process expertise you feel will be needed? Consider selecting people who are good at what you think may need to be done. Lori, for example, was looking for a team to innovate based on student input.

Pay attention to diversity and interdisciplinarity. Gender and ethnicity are important, as are experience and background. If you put four high school English teachers on a team to solve a family involvement challenge, you probably won't get the diversity of solutions you'd find with a math teacher, a parent, and a student in the mix. Strive to select people with T-shaped skills—who have a depth of experience or expertise in a particular area (represented by the vertical line in the letter T) as well as a knack for collaborating with experts in other areas (represented by the horizonal line in the letter T). In sum, pick smart, empathetic people.

Choose people who can fulfill different key roles on the team. In my design thinking course for school leaders, I ask the students on design teams to identify who will fulfill different key of roles on their team (see figure 1.1). For example:

- *Editor*—good with details and willing to make final checks on anything written the team produces.
- *Voice*—good communicating with groups and able to speak for the team.

Figure 1.1 Design team roles worksheet

WORSHEET   KICKOFF PHASE

Design Team Key Roles

Editor
Good with details and willing to make final checks on anything written which the team produces.

NAME

Voice
Good at communicating with groups and able to speak for the team.

NAME

Anchor
Methodical; can slow things down when needed.

NAME

Eavesdropper
Listens to and captures all of the team's work and asks key clarifying questions.

NAME

The Fifth Person
Asks the last question in every meeting; plays the devil's advocate.

NAME

Taskmaster
Sets objectives and outlines for the team's meetings; keeps the team focused on the schedule and the objectives.

NAME

- *Anchor*—methodical; can slow things down when needed.
- *Eavesdropper*—listens to and captures all of the team's work and asks key clarifying questions.
- *The fifth person*—askes the last question in every meeting; plays the devil's advocate.
- *Taskmaster*—sets objectives and outlines for the team's meetings; keeps the team focused on the schedule and the objectives.

Advice on Creating a Great Team

Teams tend to find this phase very rewarding. At this stage team members are just getting to know each other, and this often means a lot of friendly jockeying is taking place. They are just starting to get a sense of the broad challenge, so they will be offering their ideas on potential directions. This is natural—we all bring a wealth of experience to a team and it's only reasonable that we'd share our thoughts. This part of the design process is often a productive struggle. Each group member comes from a different place and brings different ideas and context to the table. Seeing those things collectively come to the forefront can be really satisfying.

Because design teams are diverse by design, some find that the most gratifying part at this stage is the opportunity to connect with new teammates they may know from their school or community but have never collaborated with. Dan Ryder, education director of the Success and Innovation Center at Mt. Blue High School in Maine, has brought design thinking to bear in his classroom with deliberate intent for over five years now. He employs the process to do everything from exploring literary analysis through a design lens, like asking students to empathize with the characters in John Steinbeck's *Of Mice and Men* so as to design a home that will meet their needs, to student-designed 3D-printed fidget toys that help students with anxiety and stress. When he thinks about who should be part of a design team, there's an immediate connection in his mind to the empathy component of design thinking. The first question he asks himself is, Who is experiencing a problem and what sort of pain is that problem causing them?

The second question follows from the first: Who has a vested interest in helping solve this problem? For Dan, the kind of people he'd like to see on a design team are those who recognize there's a problem—often this means bringing on team members who are experiencing the very problem he hopes to solve. It's important to design *with* users rather than *for* users when possible. This includes working shoulder to shoulder with students on a team.

General Tips for Team Effectiveness

As you have now figured out, the design team will be working closely together across the design cycle to make great things happen in your school. Here are six general tips to help make your teamwork effective.

1. Outline specific tasks that need to be done and initially allow people to volunteer for them.
2. Realize that at the beginning, team members may have formal roles in the project, but as things move forward, roles may become more fluid and start to change with the needs of the team.
3. Be polite but firm about setting deadlines and sticking to them.
4. Use some of the interview techniques you will learn in this book to uncover user needs in the team meetings. Dive deep each time a team member offers a thought or discusses an aspect of the project. Ask "why" a lot.
5. Let the natural skills of the team members be an asset to staying on track. For instance, if one of your team members is a skilled taskmaster, maybe ask that person to consider the expectations for each stage of the design cycle beforehand so as to keep the team as prepared as possible.
6. Hold a wrap-up session at the end of each team meeting to review what has been done, what the next steps are, and who will be responsible for what.

When Jesse Bacon, principal of Simons Middle School in Kentucky, formed a design team to explore personalized learning, he opened it up to teachers and staff who wanted to be a part of it. Here's how he described the start-up:

> We called it in an innovation team. I sent an email to the school community in which I set the stage for what the work of the group was

going to be. We knew that we wanted to tackle the idea of personalized learning and our hunch was we had an opportunity to address it through the school schedule. At our core, we knew we wanted to look at restructuring how we approached our work with students. While we had done a lot of work with our curriculum in developing assessments and aligning it to standards, and developing professional learning communities in the school, what was missing was a hard look at the student experience—we really wanted to look at [that]. In an email I described what the time commitment was going to be like and what the nature of the work was going to be because I wanted to make sure folks knew what they were signing up for when they decided to be a part of the team. I received just enough applications to form a team of seven: me, the vice principal and five teachers.

ASSESS YOUR SCHOOL CULTURE FOR DESIGN THINKING

Once your team is formed, the next step involves determining the school's culture and whether it is well aligned to take on design thinking as a strategy for change. Use the tool "Readiness Assessment for Design Thinking in Our School" to drive a conversation within the team about how well the norms present within your school will support a design thinking approach (see figure 1.2). Using the readiness assessment, team members reflect on how well their school norms and behaviors are aligned with the key norms and behaviors needed for the different phases of design thinking, and assign "green," "yellow," and "red" depending on the level of alignment.

When educators use the readiness assessment, they gain upfront insight on opportunities and threats that exist in their school and how they might lay the groundwork to prepare others for the work ahead. For example, design teams from schools within the Fleming County Schools district in Flemingsburg, Kentucky, used the readiness assessment to assess where risks and opportunities resided as they were about to embark on using design thinking to tackle challenges in their school. An initial and important insight—which the readiness assessment revealed—was how each team's outlook toward school change was different from that of colleagues who were not on the design team.

It may come as no surprise that in every school, each staff member's predisposition toward change falls somewhere on a continuum between acceptance and resistance. In my experience the educators who are interested in design thinking as a strategy for change tend not only to be accepting of change, but also to have an intrinsic need to encourage or lead change. This was the case for the design teams in Fleming County, which were composed entirely of change-inclined school leaders and teachers. Using the readiness assessment forced the teams to confront their own desires to move quickly for changes in their schools and consider those changes in light of how the rest of the staff might feel.

One team gave themselves yellow lights for the statements "We have norms in our school for working collaboratively" and "We have a working style that makes it easy to work on collaborative projects across classrooms or grade levels" because they realized, as a design team, they themselves were quite collaborative. But across grades and classrooms? Not so much. Because they recognized they were a team of change-inclined people, they were able to talk about how they could better focus on a culture of readiness to collaborate. They noticed that as a design team they had focused on building relationships with students, but had overlooked the importance of building relationships with all teachers and staff. This realization spurred the principal, who was a member of the design team, to consider new ways she could give all teachers a voice in the change process.

A design team from another school in Fleming County was also composed of change-inclined educators. They also had given themselves yellow lights for those two statements ("We have norms in our school for working collaboratively" and "We have a working style that makes it easy to work on collaborative projects across classrooms or grade levels"). The readiness assessment spurred an honest conversation among the team members about whether everyone on the team believes everyone in the school respects and values one another. They agreed to set aside time to brainstorm ways they could value every person in their building, even the naysayers, by finding ways to give all a voice in setting the school's direction (right down to how each could make more personal connections with colleagues they didn't know very well).

The readiness assessment also helped the design teams confront the ways in which they had included others in their planning. For instance, yet another design team from Fleming gave themselves a yellow light for "We have a culture in our school that values the opinions of noneducators (students, parents, paraprofessionals)." While they felt they collaborated well as educators in their school, when they faced up to how they had been designing a schoolwide behavior plan, they realized that, as a school, they were perhaps not as empathetic as they could be toward the students the policy would be aimed at, as they lacked a real understanding of what life at school and at home is really like for students with behavior disorders. For instance, they realized parents' views had not been considered. The readiness assessment forced the team to interrogate their own positions as school planners and policy makers, which caused them to slow down and consider how using steps in a design process could improve the way they supported students.

At another school the design team began to wonder out loud how well they really understood their students, parents, teachers, and staff when they gave a yellow light to "Staff members actively work to understand the needs of others (e.g., students, parents, peers) by hearing their stories, observing what they do, or paying attention to relevant research." The school had a culture wherein a great number of paper-and-pencil surveys were deployed throughout the year to hear from students, parents, and staff, but that data tended to just stay on the page. The readiness assessment helped the design team conceive of ways they could go beyond collecting data and ask the community about what was in the data, using questions like "Talk to us about why you think this is the case" or "Why do these issues feel important to the school?"

I recommend keeping the results from the first readiness assessment in a file and revisiting those findings periodically, particularly after running the assessment again after time has passed and the design team has begun its work. In doing so teams can assess progress on key norms and behaviors they're hoping to improve upon. Further, when progress on parts of the project seems sluggish, using the readiness assessment as a check-in can provide insights on where cultural repairs may need to be done.

Following is a list of materials you will need for your school readiness assessment.

Materials and Time Needed for the Readiness Assessment

- One readiness assessment (figure 1.2) for each team member
- Time needed for this step: 45 minutes

To use the readiness assessment, all members of the design team independently complete the protocol. Team members then discusses their responses. This can open up a discussion about where people agree and don't agree. The following questions can be used to guide the discussion:

1. For which steps or phases do we already have robust culture, practices, or programs in place?
2. How can we build on our strengths as we integrate the process into our daily work?
3. At which step or phase do we need to work on our culture?
4. How well do we think the school is doing at the tasks in each step of the process?

Debrief this discussion by creating a list of issues raised about the school's approach to using design thinking to foster change.

When asked how he believes educators should frame design thinking in their minds, Dan Ryder of Mt. Blue High School recommends viewing it as a collection of mind-sets that one adopts in order to solve problems people are facing. For example, when engaging in design thinking, you're prepared to "fail up" (a concept introduced by author and actor Leslie Odom Jr.), where you don't let fear of failure or fear of rejection diminish your spirit.[5] For Dan, design thinking is about a willingness to try things you've never tried before, and ultimately be okay with the messiness—what his best friend, educator Jeff Bailey, likes to refer to as "leaning into the squish." Design thinking is about displaying a "yes, and . . . ?" mentality, like that of an improvisational actor. It's about putting the mind-set ahead of materials, focusing on what you have (not on what you don't have). It's about focusing on meeting needs, not about being right. These are the mind-sets that Dan believes educators should

Figure 1.2 Readiness assessment for design thinking in our school

Think about the extent to which the following norms or behaviors are present at your school. Then circle R for red, Y for yellow, or G for green without talking to or peeking at your neighbors. Vote from your own experience and perspective, knowing that other people may have different experiences. The most important thing, however, is that you are able to cite evidence or an example to support your response.

RED   We **don't really do** this or **aren't really like** this.

YELLOW We **"sort of" do** this or **are like** this (it happens in pockets or inconsistently).

GREEN   We **really do** this and do it consistently or **are really like** this consistently.

PHASE	SUPPORTIVE NORMS OR BEHAVIORS	RED / YELLOW / GREEN (Have an example in mind to justify your rating)		
Kickoff	We have norms in our school for working collaboratively.	R	Y	G
	We have a working style which makes it easy to work on collaborative projects across classrooms or grade levels.	R	Y	G
	We think in terms of how something we create (a policy, practice, etc.) will make students' lives better (instead of meeting a regulation).	R	Y	G
Need finding	Staff members actively work to understand the needs of others (e.g. students, parents, peers) by hearing their stories, observing what they do, or paying attention to relevant research.	R	Y	G
	We have a culture in our school which values the opinions of non-educators (students, parents, paraprofessionals).	R	Y	G
Brainstorming	Our culture values staff members' hunches.	R	Y	G
	We're not constrained by worries that our ideas will seem trivial or "never work" here.	R	Y	G
Prototyping and testing ideas	We can test out our hunches to find out if they will work.	R	Y	G
	We let students, parents, and staff see our ideas before they are done.	R	Y	G
	We have a culture that says, "We take feedback well and can improve from it."	R	Y	G

Adapted from Boudett, Katheryn Parker, Elizabeth City, and Richard Murnane. "Stoplight Protocol Instructions." Harvard Education Press, https://datawise.gse.harvard.edu/files/datawise /files/stoplight_protocol_instructions.pdf.

possess as they tackle a challenge with design thinking. They are akin to the norms and behaviors listed in the readiness assessment.

CREATE A CHALLENGE

The next step in the process is to identify a specific challenge the design team will address. Following are three tools you can use to create your challenge: Dreams and Gripes, Choose One Challenge, and Build a Challenge Brief.

Dreams and Gripes

In many cases, design challenges emanate from a wish that something were better. In my experience, IDEO's tool to uncover dreams and gripes works well to reveal what this wish is.[6] These are the materials you will need for Dreams and Gripes:

Materials and Time Needed for Dreams and Gripes
- Dreams and Gripes worksheet (figure 1.3)
- Chart paper or a whiteboard
- Markers
- Time needed for this step: 45 minutes

Follow this process for identifying potential challenges you could address as a team:

First, have each design team member partner with one or two other team members. Using the worksheet, write down three wishes you have for the school. Phrase the wishes by filling in the following sentence: "I really wish our school had ____." Next, write down three gripes, or complaints, you have about the school. Phrase the gripes by filling in the following sentence: "It annoys me that we're not ____."

Now, flip each of the six sentences your small group developed into design challenges by turning them into "How Might We . . . ?" questions. This converts each of your dreams and gripes into design opportunities. For example, the dream "I wish we had more time for students to move about physically" turns into "How might we make more time in the day for students to move about?"

Figure 1.3 Dreams and Gripes worksheet

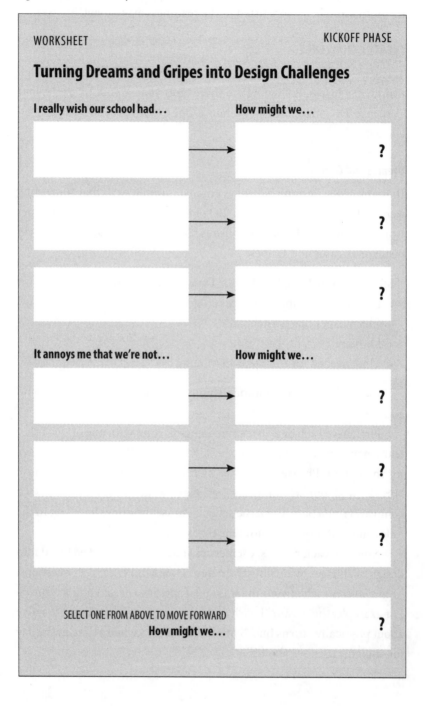

Return to the design team and review all the "How Might We . . . ?" questions that were developed. In discussing them, combine any that seem similar and refine any that need adjustments. Write your final "How Might We . . . ?" questions on a whiteboard or poster paper.

Choose One Challenge

You are now ready to narrow the field to a challenge the team would like to tackle. Remember, this is but one challenge you will try to address. Don't feel bad for not addressing them all. You can come to others in turn. These are the materials you will need:

Materials and Time Needed for Choose One Challenge
- List of "How Might We . . . ?" options
- Chart paper or a whiteboard
- Markers
- Colored adhesive dots (one color is fine)
- Time needed for this step: 45 minutes

Good challenges have six features, so consider these as you refine the challenge statements and move toward selecting one to work on:[7]

1. They are fairly simple. A reasonable person could grasp what you are trying to accomplish on a first read.
2. They are optimistic. They imbue a sense of a positive future if the challenge is solved.
3. They are broad enough to discover something unexpected. If the challenge is too narrow, then the result may be preordained. Never embed potential solutions inside a "How Might We . . . ?" question. For instance, "How might we create a professional development program using electronic tablets to address objective 2.1 of our math standards?" presumes that solving a challenge in math instruction requires professional development, tablets, and a focus on a specific math standard. This deleteriously constrains the design work.
4. At the same time, they are narrow enough to make the topic manageable. A challenge like "How might we improve teaching and learning here?" is too broad and unwieldy.

5. The challenge need not be to create something new. It's perfectly reasonable to redesign something that already exists. As my colleague Larry Leifer of Stanford University likes to say, "All design is redesign." Or as Salvador Dali said, "Those who do not want to imitate anything, produce nothing."

6. The challenge is associated with readily understandable measures of success. For example, in the case of a challenge pertaining to the school schedule, measures like attendance, tardies, absentee rates, or school liking could be used.

Keep in mind the timing or length of the challenge. The nice thing about schools is they run on a fairly well-defined calendar. The semester, quarter, marking period, and so on make for nicely defined periods of time when you know people will be in the school and available. Thus, I recommend your forays extend along a semester or yearlong timeline. For beginning efforts, a semester is a good time frame. It's long enough to give teams time to work out any adjustments in a design cycle, but short enough to drive urgency and creativity as you march toward solution sets.

To select a challenge for your team, try dot voting. Place on the wall the list of possible "How Might We . . . ?" challenges you created in the last step. Each design team member places one to three dots next the challenges they would like the team to work on. No team member may place more than three dots on any challenge. The challenge with the most dots is selected.

Build a Challenge Brief

The final tool in this section is the challenge brief. The challenge brief is the team's first public work product. It's a simple, yet powerful document that enables those outside the team to understand the challenge you'll undertake. It consists of just two or three sentences that cover the *context,* the *problem,* and the *opportunity.* For example, let's say you were writing a challenge brief to address teacher data literacy. Context and problem are addressed in the first sentence, and opportunity is addressed in the second and third sentences. Here's a challenge brief in full; then we'll break it down part by part.

With the time for teacher professional development dwindling, and increasing pressure to use data to improve teaching and learning, teachers feel constrained in their ability to improve their craft. The day pattern strongly influences how teacher work occurs. There is a big opportunity to redesign the day pattern to better address the professional learning needs of our teachers.

Now let's break that down.

Context: "With the time for teacher professional development dwindling, and increasing pressure to use data to improve teaching and learning . . ."

Problem: ". . . teachers feel constrained in their ability to improve their craft."

Opportunity: "The day pattern strongly influences how teacher work occurs. There is a big opportunity to redesign the day pattern to better address the professional learning needs of our teachers."

Use figure 1.4 to build your challenge brief. For this process, you will need the following materials:

Materials and Time Needed for Building the Challenge Brief
- Final "How Might We . . . ?" question
- Challenge brief worksheet (figure 1.4)
- Pens
- Time needed for this step: 30 minutes

To build your brief, you can work either as a large group or in smaller groups. Once you have finished, you should notice how you were able to develop a concise statement of the challenge with just enough context, feeling, and opportunity to let others react in a constructive way. Circulate the brief among stakeholders in the school, including likely users, and take in their reactions. Remember, throughout the process any work product of the team is not precious. It's the feedback you receive that's the gold. It's rare to get the challenge right the first time, and as you enter into the next chapter and phase on need finding, it may morph a bit. Be open to the idea

Figure 1.4 Challenge brief worksheet

WORKSHEET   KICKOFF PHASE

Build a Challenge Brief

❶ Enter the "How might we…?" question selected by the team that represents the challenge to be worked on. E.g., How might we reimagine the day pattern (school schedule) to enhance teacher professional development?

❷ Draft the first phrase of the brief: the context. E.g., "With the time for teacher professional development dwindling, and increasing pressure to use data to improve teaching and learning…"

❸ Draft the second phrase of the brief: the problem. E.g., "…teachers feel constrained in their ability to improve their craft."

❹ Draft the third phrase of the brief: the opportunity. E.g., "The day pattern strongly influences how teacher work occurs. There is a big opportunity to redesign the day pattern to better address the professional learning needs of our teachers."

❺ Write the entire brief here.

❻ Share the brief with stakeholders. Ask if the challenge described is:
☐ Optimistic   ☐ Simple to understand   ☐ Narrow enough to manage
☐ Broad enough to allow for unexpected discoveries
☐ Has measures of success associated with it

---

that your challenge will shift as it is exposed to stakeholders. For instance, my colleague Dan Gilbert and I worked with the principal and a group of students from Rowan County High School in Morehead, Kentucky. The principal and the members of a young women's leadership group at the school had been discussing for some time the perceived impact popular media may be having on girls' self-concept around body image. In a workshop where members of the community were enlisted for the design team, students, faculty, and leaders from Rowan County schools were empathetically interviewed as part of a need finding effort on this challenge. As the challenge was unpacked during the interviews it also shifted. The challenge changed to one that was more salient and closer to a root issue. It moved from a question of "How might we help young women improve self-image in light of popular media's notions of ideal body image?" to "How might we enhance the interpersonal relationships between young women in high school?" The students, in particular, were instrumental in helping the team navigate this shift. Fundamentally, an issue that emanates from popular media is a difficult one to solve. However, helping young women form strong relationships with each other and not propagating media tropes about "how I should look" became feasible to address.

The team should have a strong opinion that is weakly held about the initial challenge. This is because the challenge is, more likely than not, going to change over time as you learn more about it during the need finding phase. Remember, that is the nature of a wicked problem: you don't know what the problem really is until you begin trying to solve it. Be open to adjusting the brief, or even coming up with new challenge ideas thanks to the reactions you receive on the brief.

POTENTIAL OBSTACLES IN THE KICKOFF PHASE

Do obstacles arise in the first phases of the design process? Yes. For instance, it can be a challenge to maintain a fresh perspective at this point and not make assumptions or predictions about your users or the solutions you will develop. Trust me when I say, "Trust the process." I've met many educational leadership graduate students who, being new to design thinking, find it difficult to resist coming up with an immediate solution without first truly understanding the problem. They become a bit frustrated when, say, in the need finding stage, I ask them to temper their opinions on how to solve the problems they are learning about. They are, after all, educators and are trained to solve problems. But I continue to implore them to trust the process—the steps for problem solving will arrive, I tell them. And invariably, they later say they wish they had just trusted the process because they realize it works—solutions do arrive. Embracing ambiguity is hard, but essential. The light anxiety my graduate students feel when they aren't allowed to jump to solutions is precisely the feeling one gets when one *leans into the squish*. In the early stages of a design cycle a lot of information is coming at the team from users and others. If, in those early stages, everyone starts brainstorming a solution to what they believe to be the problem, it's a sign they need to slow down—teams need to take a step back, trust the process, and resist the urge to offer solutions right away. Don't be lulled into a sense of satisfaction just because you feel your team members are working well together and therefore can come up with good ideas on their own—they must empathize with the people they are designing for. If they don't, the ideas the team comes up with mean nothing.

It is sometimes hard to not jump ahead of the process and start getting into the weeds of planning what you think will best meet the needs of the users. You really have to take yourself out of it and embrace the role of observer and gatherer of info.

Some members of the team may have a deep knowledge about the challenge you will take on and others may have none at all. Let those people be a guide in the areas where they have expertise.

There can also be challenges in deciding how you want to orient yourselves as a team. While it's important to have diversity in the design team and to assign roles to team members that play to their respective strengths, you should also recognize that there may be quite a bit of crossover in responsibilities and a diversity of opinions on how those responsibilities should be carried out. Team members should acknowledge these differences as advantages rather than interpret certain actions as stepping on toes. One graduate student I worked with said of her team,

"Something I feel could have been done differently was to ask more questions and have fewer ideas."

HOW TO BE EFFECTIVE AT THE KICKOFF PHASE

Try these ideas to make the kickoff phase more effective:

- Schedule a regular time to meet. The best time will obviously depend on team members' schedules. Some teams are able to have a common planning time before or after school. Once team members have their charge, some may meet in smaller groups as needed. For instance, if teachers on the team already meet regularly for PD, they might use part of that time for design team work.
- Consider using a collaborative online document where team members can write down ideas before meetings. This could be in a shared Google Doc on Google Drive or a shared Microsoft Word document on Microsoft OneDrive.
- Hold a design team meeting simply to understand the challenge— it's an effective way to understand team member strengths as well as get everyone on the same page. Ask the following questions of each team member to help refine the initial challenge statement.[8]
  - What are your initial thoughts about the challenge topic?
  - What barriers or constraints do you see?
  - What do you know about the challenge topic?
  - What would you like to learn more about?
- Take stock at the outset of what all the steps in a design process entail. This way each member of the team can begin to think in terms of their role on the team and frame their contributions in light of their strengths.

WHAT'S NEXT?

This chapter has taken you through the kickoff phase of the design process and prepared you for the next step, which is need finding. In need finding, you and your teammates will embark on an exciting and inspiring journey of empathy, learning a great deal about what makes the users in your challenge tick.

CHAPTER **2**

NEED FINDING

The innovation team met to talk about the next phase of the design cycle—to gain empathy and discover unmet needs among the students at Jackson Elementary. Team members elected to start small by focusing chiefly on interviews as their method for discovery. Lori Mills, the principal, explained her desire to have the team select students to interview who represented a wide sampling of the student body. Sandra, a fourth-grade teacher, offered a suggestion: "We have a lot of children who are daughters and sons of teachers not only in this building, but across the district. They would be an accessible group of students to interview."

"Thank you, Sandra," Lori said before expanding on the suggestion. "Our teachers' children are accessible—but at the same time I don't want to be lulled into a false sense of security that we can rely on interviewing the most accessible kiddos. We have a whole new population of English language learners here in our school, and we need to make sure they are included. We also have students in two highly structured classrooms, and we want to make sure their input is valued. Plus we have students with emotional/behavior disorders, and we want those kids included."

Pete, a fifth-grade teacher, concurred. "You're right. If we just hit the population of kids we have access to all the time, we won't get a true feeling of what's actually happening."

Once the team settled on a diverse set of students to interview, Lori knew that the team would need a set of prompts designed to drive a conversation with Jackson Elementary's students that would move them beyond just talking. They needed prompts that would not only elicit great responses, but also make teachers really listen. Lori explained this in an innovation team meeting, and members created a list of questions that they would ask in each of their interviews with students.

Pete spoke up. "I feel like we do a good job of talking to kids but as far as tracking what's being said or getting information that we can use, that just doesn't happen day to day—we don't have a process to handle it. I mean, our kids here know me, and they are not afraid to talk to me, but it's not as meaningful as it could be." Pete thought for a moment before continuing. "I think an additional aspect to this is that adults in a school are used to speaking to the kids, but they are not used to pausing and really hearing them."

Samantha, another fourth-grade teacher, said, "You know, in about every successful business there is an effort to put a focus on the customer— but not in schools. We don't really seek the voice of the customer, our kids. Don't get me wrong, we care for them, keep them safe, and teach them as best we can, but we don't ever ask them what we can do better. If we want to change, we have to move beyond meeting the regulatory needs of the state and look to how we can meet the human needs of the kids."

Lori, the principal, concurred. "Yes," she said, and then asked the team, "How can we have them codesign, with us, their learning experience and not just be the product of a learning experience?"

The next phase in the design cycle is need finding. Need finding is just what it sounds like—finding what people need. This is not about determining physical things one might buy, but finding out how they need the world to be arranged so they can succeed, how they want to feel when they engage in particular activities, and why they love certain things, situations, or environments and can't stand others. It is an act of really hearing others.[1] It's a process of discovery.[2] It's a time to be user-centered and focus on the emotional experiences your users have in the environments within which you are designing. In this phase you'll embark on a series of conversations and observations that are designed to transform the way you see your school and the students, teachers, staff, and parents who are a part of it. The findings from these conversations and observations will be synthesized into a profile of those you are designing for—your "users." And with that profile you will be able to design solutions to the challenges people in your school are facing.

Effective need finding requires that you adopt a beginner's mind-set. Your head is filled with an array of beliefs brought about by the wealth of experiences you've had in your life. Furthermore, any professional training you've had has provided you with frameworks for thinking as well as some analytical tools. These are very valuable assets to have as a designer, but shouldn't be brought to bear in this phase. Later, as you begin to synthesize information, plan implementation, and judge success, your skills will be helpful. But in this phase, your existing ideas can prejudice what you hear and see. Therefore, adopt a beginner's mind-set. Enter this phase with a level of naïveté so you can see the world from your users' eyes. This can be hard to do, but the payoff can be big. Bruce Mau, a well-respected design thinker, said, "The fear for so many people is that, in asking these kinds of questions, they will seem naïve. But being naïve is a valuable commodity in this context. Naïveté is what allows you to try to do what the experts say can't be done."[3] Here are four tips on how to adopt a beginner's mind-set.[4]

1. *Don't judge.* Merely observe what you are seeing and hearing without placing any value or judgment on it.
2. *Question everything.* Be as naïve as a four-year-old. You should especially question things you think you already understand. If you are doing an interview, treat your user as an expert and ask the person "why" a lot (see the five-whys technique below).
3. *Be truly curious.* Enter every environment, even those you are very familiar with, from a position of wonder and curiosity.

4. *Really, really listen.* Lose yourself in what users say to you and how they say it.

Keep in mind that need finding is a different activity, philosophically and practically, from conducting a needs assessment. Therefore, avoid using surveys. I run into quite a few people new to design thinking who, when they get to this phase, want to send out a survey to people they feel represent their users. But honestly, surveys rarely have a place in this process. Design thinking is not a statistical process. And surveys are not structured to allow design team members to follow up in the moment. For instance, you can't effectively apply the five-whys technique in a survey. I strongly discourage my students from using surveys in the need finding phase.

As you and your team enter this phase I also recommend you lower your standards. This tip may sound a bit counterintuitive. What I mean is, don't worry if you feel as though you have not talked to all the people you could have interviewed, observed all the settings you might have visited, or asked all the questions in your mind. Don't worry if you feel like you could cover more ground with a survey (read the preceding paragraph again). You will have plenty of chances in subsequent phases to ask more question and get more information. Even though this phase is called need finding, in truth you will also be engaged in forms of need finding in the prototyping, feedback, and implementation phases. Because the goal of design thinking implies addressing unmet needs, you should always be checking in with your users in all the phases.

In this phase you will select users to interview and observe so as to better understand their lives and discover their unmet needs. My recommendation is that you select users from the extremes. The need finding phase of a design cycle is the foundation for generating inspiration within the design team as they seek solutions to problems facing users. Inspiration often comes when, in the process of talking with or observing someone, you discover their work-arounds or novel approaches to dealing with the world.[5] This means that engaging with the right kind of people is important from the outset. Engaging users who are on the "extremes" of a challenge will help you discover meaningful needs that may arise in interactions with people in the middle. Interestingly, the needs of extreme users are often also the needs of those across the spectrum. To choose extreme users, think about the challenge you are addressing and how people might fall along a spectrum of engagement relative to the challenge. For instance, if you have a hunch that the school schedule affects stakeholders in your school, you might consider factors like these: how students get to school, how teachers get to school, which students work, which students are themselves parents, and the absentee rates of students. If you were examining the issue of absentee rates, you might talk to students who are chronically absent, students who are always absent at certain times of the day, students who are never absent, and so forth.

Jesse Bacon, the principal at Simons Middle School, for example, and his "innovation team" decided to interview a large sample of a hundred students from their 327-member student body in their desire to explore possible ways to increase personalized learning. Their initial hunch was that there was an opportunity to create a more flexible school schedule so students could go to classes they needed when they needed them. The team strived to sample from across the population. Among the one hundred were students who participated in the free and reduced-price lunch program, students with special needs, students who had good grades, and students who did not. A balance was sought across gender lines as well. The innovation team talked to all one hundred students, with each of the seven innovation team members talking to about fifteen students each over the course of a month. All the team members jumped in to conduct an interview whenever they could, be it during their planning period, over lunch, before school, or after school.

There are a number of approaches you can use to help identify the needs of users. In this chapter, I present three approaches that work well in schools: empathetic interviews, shadow safaris, and photo studies. Any one of these tools—or a combination of them—will yield a rich set of findings that can take you to the next step of crafting a character composite. Here are some thoughts on using these procedures under different situations.

If you have to choose only one of the approaches below and the users in the challenge are grade four or higher or are educators, parents, or other stakeholders, I recommend the empathetic interview. Empathetic interviews support positive relationships between educators and students and between adults. They are the go-to tool for nearly every school-based design team I've worked with.

If the users are young children, say grade three and lower, you can still use empathetic interviewing, but I recommend augmenting those conversations with a shadow safari or a user photo study. Children in the second or third grade can often carry on a rich conversation based on the interview protocol I offer in this book, but kids between the ages of four and six may not open up as much as older classmates. That's why adding a shadowing component can be useful so you can observe what children do and how they do it. Asking parents to help with a photo study is one way you can accumulate pictures of a young student's life. The photos can then be used to preface a series of empathetic questions about what's in the image and why the student likes what's in it.

If time permits, I encourage you to use all three approaches in the need finding stage. The interviews will provide you with surprising, useful findings and rich quotations from users as well as build important trust with the users. The shadow safari will provide context to the interviews by giving the team a chance to affirm whether what they hear in the interviews is occurring in the school setting, as well as reveal new insights that were not disclosed in the interviews. And the photo study gives the team a glimpse into the mind's eye of the user, which opens up a new world of questions that can be asked based on the photos that are taken.

Each of these will yield information that, when synthesized, will contribute to the making of an overarching story of your users and, in turn, to the creation of one or more character composites that will be needed in the following phases.

EMPATHETIC INTERVIEWS

The empathetic interview is the staple of the need finding and empathy stage of a design thinking process. One tool I really like is the IDEO three-part interview method, *Start Specific, Go Broad, Probe Deep.*[6] Why? This tool allows a novice designer to have a meaningful conversation with users that puts the users at ease, explores their wants and desires in a nonthreatening way, and allows for deep exploration of the challenge at hand. Let's look at each part in turn.

Start Specific. The idea here is to build rapport with the person you are interviewing by beginning with questions that are easy for them to answer. In doing so, you may begin to hear them use some jargon that will give you insight into their life.

Go Broad. Before stepping into questions about the challenge at hand, open up the space for your user to talk about their hopes and aspirations and if they perceive of anything that could get in the way. Understanding this broader context of what they want out of life provides valuable insight on how to contextualize the responses they'll give when you probe deeper into the challenge.

Probe Deep. It's only now, in this last part of the interview, that you discuss with any specificity the challenge at hand. This may seem paradoxical, leaving the conversation about the challenge to the end. However, starting here without first asking easy questions and then discussing some broader aspirations or goals tends to result in conversations about the challenge that are less rich and lead to diminished insights. In this phase of the interview, ask questions that bear directly on the challenge. And don't keep your agenda a secret—this is not a test. It's okay to tell the person you're interviewing what your aim is and what you'd like to know. The user is, after all, your partner in this effort.

The example of an empathetic interview protocol in the sidebar explores the challenge of creating student-centered schooling in middle school using the Start Specific, Go Broad, Probe Deep tool.

The following step-by-step guide will help you use the Start Specific, Go Broad, Probe Deep tool to create and implement an empathetic interview tailored to address your challenge. There are five steps in this process: create the interview protocol, identify the interview team, identify the interviewees, conduct the interviews, and capture your thoughts.

Step 1: Create the Interview Protocol

Use the conversation builder worksheet in figure 2.1 to help you create a protocol for the interview. This protocol is modeled after the example in the sidebar and should be modified to meet the needs of your challenge.

Example of an Empathetic Interview

START SPECIFIC

1. What grade are you in?
2. How long have you been at your school?
3. What kinds of things do you think you do differently from kids in other grades?

GO BROAD

4. What are your aspirations for the future?
5. Why did you choose those?
6. What do you see that could get in the way of achieving your goals? (This could be anything—not necessarily school-related.)

PROBE DEEP

Tell the student: We want to figure out how to put you at the center of the way your school teaches. We want to teach you in a way that is specifically tailored to your needs.

7. What's the biggest problem currently in your school (or class, grade, etc.)?
   (After the response, ask, "Why do you say that?")
8. What do you wish the teachers knew but don't about students?
   (After the response, ask, "Why do you say that?")
9. What do you wish the principal at school knew but doesn't?
   (After the response, ask, "Why do you say that?")
10. If you could give the teachers some advice, what would it be?
    (After the response, ask, "Why do you say that?")
11. If you had a week to spend learning whatever you wanted at school, what would that be?
    (After the response, ask, "Why do you say that?")
12. Based on the responses, make up an idea you think the student would love. Test it out on them. For example, "What if your school did _____? Would you like that?" Follow with: "Why do you say that?"

Step 2: Identify the Interview Team

When conducting interviews, have two members from the design team participate, one to ask the questions and one to write everything down.

Step 3: Identify the Interviewees

In considering how many users to interview at a time, one-on-one conversations work best. Remember to be thoughtful in selecting a variety of users across the entire continuum of people in your user group. Be particularly purposeful in choosing users who are at the extremes of

Figure 2.1 Interview protocol worksheet

WORKSHEET   NEED FINDING PHASE

Conversation Builder

Start Specific

Write some questions that will start to build rapport with the interviewee. Create questions that are easy to answer. In doing so, you may begin to hear them use some jargon that will give you insight into their life.

Go Broad

Write some questions that will prompt your user to talk about their hopes and aspirations and anything they feel might get in the way of those. Understanding their wants and desires at this level can provide important insights that will allow you to make greater sense of their responses in the next section of the conversation.

Probe Deep

Write some questions you'd like to ask about the specific challenge at hand. Remember, it's only now that you discuss the challenge (in the first two phases of the conversation you're focused on the user, irrespective of the challenge).

the continuum. It's at those edges where the most interesting new ideas tend to be found. For example, if high school students are your users, you would want to select about a third of your conversation participants from those students who are doing very well in school, about a third who struggle or are not comfortable with school, and about a third who are in the middle of those two extremes.

Step 4: Conduct the Interviews

In this step team members will conduct interviews based on the interviewees you identified in step 3. It is strongly recommended that you conduct interviews with a partner.

Materials and Time Needed for Conducting Interviews
- Interview protocol (figure 2.1)
- Notepad
- Pen
- Time needed for this step: 30 minutes for each interview

To start the interview, explain that the purpose of the interview is to understand a particular challenge the school is facing from the user's perspective. Let them know you are suspending your own beliefs about how the world works and want to know their view. Let them know you consider them the expert of their own worldview (because they are). Write down everything you hear, and take note of any body language, facial expressions, interesting quotes, or other aspects of the conversation that surprise you.

Several tips will help keep you on track. Throughout the conversation, frequently ask "why?" The five-whys technique is a powerful tool wherein you ask the question "why?" up to five times in a row to the responses your user provides. Doing so reveals underlying thought processes and rationales for a user's beliefs. Even asking "why?" three times can be revelatory. However, asking it over and over can become repetitive (and annoying!). Here are four additional ways to ask "why?" without sounding creepy.

1. What feels critical about that?
2. Why is that, do you think?

3. Tell me more about why that's important to you.

4. I see. How so?

Be careful that you don't accidentally ask questions that presume you know how they feel. Asking, for instance, "What are three things you like about school?" presumes they like school. Instead, ask, "Can you tell me about your experiences at school?"

Step 5: Capture Your Thoughts

1. At the end of each interview, with your partner, capture your thoughts on the following while they are fresh in your mind using figure 2.2, the conversation highlights worksheet.
   - What surprised you in this interview?
   - What was a memorable quote?
   - What does this person care about?
   - What sort of things frustrate this person?
   - How do they want to feel?
   - What questions would you still like to ask?

* * *

As members of the innovation team conducted interview after interview, they began to derive insights they had never considered before about the students of Jackson Elementary. When Pete, the fifth-grade teacher, met fellow innovation team member Samantha, a fourth-grade teacher, at the school entrance one morning, she asked him how the innovation team work was going for him.

"Really enlightening," Pete said. "Yesterday I asked a boy one of my favorite questions from the conversation protocol—'What is your most memorable learning experience ever?' The boy said, 'My papaw taught me to drive a tractor,' and he went on to tell me how he learned to drive a tractor by, well, driving the tractor. And I thought to myself, he learns best from doing. He learned how to drive that tractor because he was doing it—that gives me insight on how we can help children like him learn."

Samantha shared an insight she had discovered. "I was chatting with a fourth-grade girl who, as I walked back with her to class at the end of our conversation, started dancing. I said to her, 'You're a dancer?' and she

Figure 2.2 Conversation highlights worksheet

WORKSHEET   NEED FINDING PHASE

Conversation Highlights: Fresh Thoughts

At the end of a conversation with a user, meet with your partner to capture the following findings while they are still fresh in your mind.

❶ What surprised you in this conversation?

❷ What are one or two memorable quotes that stood out in this conversation?

❸ Considering everything you talked about, what does it seem like this person cares about?

❹ What sorts of things frustrate this person?

❺ How does this person want to feel? (For instance, *safe, needed, confident*, etc.)

❻ Now that you've been able to reflect on the conversation, what are some questions you'd still like to ask?

said, 'No, I don't like to dance. I just want to move.' It's no wonder, Pete. With only one recess a day, she sits practically all day. It's stunning how many things we hear or see from the students that are so easily dismissed as superficial statements."

It's not unusual for the power of design thinking to make itself apparent when team members start interviewing students. Jesse Bacon, at Simons Middle School, for example, remembers everyone on the innovation team being surprised by how much the kids told them, and how insightful their comments were. Many of the team members said things like "I thought I knew X, but I didn't know it at all." Several team members expected they might get silly, ridiculous, or pie-in-the-sky type answers. But in the end the information received was very practical.

When having conversations with middle to upper-primary-grade children, say grades 3 through 5, it's not uncommon for questions like "What's your favorite subject" or "What would you change about the school" to elicit simple answers like "lunch" or "recess all day." Don't dismiss answers like these as silly or unrealistic. Dive in with five whys to get to the feelings behind the response. It could be a student loves lunch because she sees her friends. The social aspects of lunch can provide you with insight on how to make other parts of the learning day more engaging for her. If a student says he wants recess all day, it may be because he's restless or bored, but you'll never know unless you ask. Getting to the bottom of that may lead you to design novel solutions to the fidgeting he does in class all day. Find out how students feel and what the feelings are behind their answers. That will lead to rich opportunities for design.

Other Methods for Conducting Empathetic Interviews

The design team doesn't have to be the only group conducting interviews. Some educators have had success with students interviewing students. At Fairdale Elementary School in Louisville, Kentucky, for example, assistant principal Erin Coyle enlisted a cadre of students at neighboring Fairdale High School to empathetically converse with her young students. Having recently participated in the Next Generation Leadership Academy, an annual, multiday professional development experience for teachers and school leaders in Kentucky, Erin had learned how to apply tenets of design thinking to create a culture of codesign among students and teachers in the name of school change. She now seeks to use design thinking to better understand the needs of the students in her school. She took what she had learned in the academy training and expanded the notion of student involvement. Her approach to how students' needs would be captured was unique. Erin and Dr. Tara Issacs, director of professional learning and development in Jefferson County Public Schools (and fellow Next Generation Leadership Academy alumna), trained students enrolled in Fairdale High School's Teaching and Early Childhood Career Pathway program how to conduct empathetic interviews using a version of the protocol described in this book. Essentially, they trained future teachers on how to view schoolchildren as partners in design. Erin took into account the native languages of her elementary-age students and strived to match them with high school students who were native speakers of the same language. High school students who conducted interviews with elementary students in a language other than English translated questions on the fly from the interview protocol, which was written in English, into oral questions in their native language. Elementary students would respond in kind and responses were written down in English by the high school student. Not only did this create new opportunities for elementary and high school students to be a part of a school improvement process, but the learnings captured by the high school students were used by their teacher in the Teaching and Early Childhood Career Pathway program in a unit on integrating student voice in the classroom.

In another interesting approach to interviewing, Garth Nichols, the vice principal of Student Engagement and Experiential Development at Havergal College, an independent K–12 girls' school in Toronto, Canada, decided to have students and teachers switch roles as a part of the empathetic interview process. As a design thinker, Garth's approach to education starts with an overarching question: How can we use this design thinking approach with students to impart their meaningful, authentic voice in their own education? In this case, Garth and his school community sought to uncover solutions to the challenge posed by smartphone use in school—a challenge expressed by different stakeholders, including students, faculty, and parents. For parents, it went something like this: "I restrict my daughter's access to internet data via her personal device while at home because I'm trying to help her manage her use of social media and her overall exposure to the internet. But when she comes to school, there's not the same level of control. While there is a robust education about tech and supervision of students, they still have unlimited access to Wi-Fi. Student access to the internet is not filtered—they have unlimited access. So, how will you partner with me to help me raise my daughter in the age of the internet?"

At about the same time, a couple of provocative articles appeared in a Canadian national newspaper, the *Globe and Mail*, on research regarding the pitfalls of social media and exposure to the internet over a long period of time. Combine these two things with the results of a recent student survey indicating that Havergal could do more with its students around personal device use. Havergal elected to explore the space around personal smartphone use by students.

As a design thinker, Garth thought this was an opportunity for meaningful student engagement. He convened a group of stakeholders to be on a design team, including two students from every grade, three faculty members, and two school administrators. At the team's first meeting, Garth explained that everyone's voice on the team was equal and that empathizing with each other would be key. The first step, he said, would be for students to take on the role of teacher, and teachers to take on the role of students.

Out of those discussions, several things came to light. First was that the challenge they thought they had before them wasn't the real challenge at all. Through empathetic conversations and research, students and faculty wrestled with different perspectives—which wasn't always easy—and analyzed the policies in other schools to see how they handled the problem. Through this process, the working group uncovered biases and assumptions: students empathized with teachers and in the design process were able to walk in the teachers' shoes and begin to see how it might feel to enforce a school policy on student device use. Students said they didn't want to put their teachers in the position of being the police, confiscating devices.

And in turn, the teachers understood how it felt from the students' point of view, noting how if they were a student, they would hate to have their phone taken away and the impact that might have on their lived experience. Thus, the dialogue became more nuanced. As the conversation evolved the people in the room—students, teachers, and administrators alike—realized the challenge that had been posed was not the right challenge.

The empathetic conversations provided a platform for group members to interrogate whether their original challenge was the right question. Through shared research and design thinking protocols, they concluded it was not addressing an issue that revealed itself through the dialogue. For them, this challenge was not just a question of whole-school use of personal devices. It was a question about what activities, interactions, and behaviors the school community should value in the time available between classes (e.g., during passing periods or at the lunch hour).

SHADOW SAFARIS

A second approach to need finding is shadowing a user (who is typically a student). The purpose of shadowing users (with their permission of course) is to understand what their life is like during a typical day. Shadowing allows you to directly observe how people experience the environment within which your challenge exists. Take, for instance, the challenge of re-designing the school schedule. Shadowing a student throughout the day allows you to observe where things are working and where sticking points or areas of organizational failure are getting in the way of the student's goals.

In a shadow safari, one design team member shadows one user at a time. There is no limit on the number of design team members who can go on safaris. The following guide will help you plan and conduct a shadow safari. There are four steps in this process: identify the group of individuals you will shadow, prepare for the shadow safari, conduct the safari, and capture your thoughts.

Step 1: Identify the Shadow Group

Time is the only limiting resource in terms of how many students you should shadow. If your team is able to, shadow several students. Identify a student to shadow and obtain their permission to follow them for all or part of their day. As described earlier in this chapter, consider shadowing students who are on the margins or don't consider school to be the best experience. When recruiting students for this process, explain that your interest in shadowing them stems from wanting to learn from their experiences firsthand. Explain that you believe students are the experts of their own experiences, and in order to better design solutions to challenges they may face, you need to be able to see for yourself what their world is like.

Step 2: Prepare for the Shadow

If possible, obtain a copy of the student's schedule so you can plan your day. Use figure 2.3 to plan your safari, including a list of things you hope to learn from the student as they relate to your challenge. Clear your calendar and let coworkers and staff know you'll be out for the day. This includes leaving your walkie-talkie in the office.

Step 3: Conduct the Shadow Safari

During your shadowing time, look at everything with fresh eyes, as though you were the student you are shadowing. At the beginning of the day, let the student know you won't be too obvious (and then don't be!). Ask the student how you can best do this without making them self-conscious. Follow some distance back (like a shadow), and when in class sit a few rows away and in the background. At lunch observe from a bit away. Capture your observations via notes, photos, or quick sketches. Ask follow-up questions of your student when you have a moment between experiences if you aren't sure about the context of a situation or can't make sense of something that has occurred.

Materials and Time Needed for Conducting a Shadow Safari
- A copy of the student's schedule
- Safari planning worksheet (figure 2.3)
- Notebook to capture observations, thoughts, sketches
- Pen
- Time needed for this step: A school day

Figure 2.3 Shadow safari planning worksheet

WORKSHEET   NEED FINDING PHASE

Planning a Shadow Safari

STUDENT NAME, GRADE

What is the design challenge?

Given the design challenge topic and the student you are shadowing, what is a goal you have for the shadow experience? What do you hope to learn? What are you curious about?

Plan ahead

Who (Who might I see my student interact with? Who do I want to be sure to see my student interact with?)

What (What things might I see my student interact with? What do I want to be sure to look for?)

Where (Where are some places I might see interesting interactions?)

Why (How can I remain attuned to emotions or feelings my student might have during the day?)

Step 4: Capture Your Thoughts

At the end of shadowing, use the worksheet in figure 2.4 to capture your thoughts while they are fresh in your mind.

USER PHOTO STUDIES

The third approach to need finding is a user photo study. This tool helps you to gain deeper insight into the lives of those you are designing for. There are four steps for planning and conducting a user photo study: prepare for the study, identify the users, conduct the study, and capture your thoughts.

Step 1: Prepare for the Study

To prepare, you will create a set of instructions for the students who will be taking photos for the study, such as, "I'd like to understand what a day in your life is like. On any day you wish, take photos of experiences at home and school that feel important to you."[7] Another option is to use a process from IDEO, where teams have been known to hand out Kodak Instamatics to users with a checklist of photos to take glued to the back of the camera.[8] You can do the same sort of thing with students. Since almost every student has their own camera on their smartphone, why not hand out a preprinted index card with a couple dozen photo ideas. Then instruct your user to take pictures of the things on the list. See the sidebar for ideas of things to put on the list.

Suggestions for Pictures to Take During a User Photo Study

1. Here are three pictures of me.
2. This is my pocket or purse.
3. These are my shoes.
4. This is where I live.
5. This is where I sleep.
6. This is what I see when I step outside.
7. This is what I bought for a dollar.
8. This is my favorite drink.
9. This is my favorite food.
10. I wish I had this.
11. I spend most of my time here.
12. This is something I need.
13. This is someone I love.
14. This is where I relax.
15. I spend time with friends here.
16. This is someone I respect.
17. This is beautiful to me.
18. This is something I worry about.
19. This is something I am proud of.
20. This is something I want to improve.
21. I use this every day.

Figure 2.4 Shadow safari highlights worksheet

WORKSHEET   NEED FINDING PHASE

Shadow Safari Highlights: Fresh Thoughts

At the end of a shadow safari, capture the following while they are still fresh in your mind.

STUDENT NAME, GRADE

❶ What surprised you about what you observed or heard?

❷ What are one or two memorable quotes or scenes that stood out in this observation?

❸ Considering everything you talked about, what does it seem like this person cares about?

❹ What sorts of things frustrate this person?

❺ How does this person want to feel? (For instance, *safe*, *needed*, *confident*, etc.)

❻ Now that you've been able to reflect on the observation, what are some questions you'd still like to ask or scenes you'd like to observe?

Step 2: Identify the Users

Identify a few users you would like to know more about and ask them if they would be willing to take photographs of their day. As with the other tools, it is best to identify users who represent the extremes or are from "the edges." For instance, if the team is addressing a design challenge that relates to student transportation to school, you might want to choose some students who walk to school, some who take the bus, and some who ride in a car. If the design challenge is about food at school, you wouldn't want to have only those students who eat in the cafeteria. You would want to involve students who may not eat at all, or are food insecure, or who bring their own food each day. Strive to have one third from either extreme of the continuum of potential users and about one third from the center.

Step 3: Conduct the User Study

Notify the users when they can begin their photo study. Give users a timeline for when you would like to receive their photos and the format, such as uploading to a specific site or sending via email.

Step 4: Capture Your Thoughts

There are two parts to the capture process: user interview and team member discussion. First, set up a time to meet with the students to look over the photos together. I recommend that two design team members hold one conversation per user (don't bring them all in at once to discuss their pictures together).

You will need about thirty minutes for this task. First, ask them about each photo they took and to tell you either (a) more about the what's in the photo and (b) how they felt about what's captured in the photo. Use your five whys to explore deeper.

Second, after the user interview is complete, team members capture their thoughts on the following while they are fresh using figure 2.2.

- What surprised you in this interview?
- What was a memorable quote?
- What does this person care about?

- What sort of things frustrate this person?
- How do they want to feel?
- What questions would you still like to ask?

Materials and Time Needed for Conducting User Photo Studies
- A quiet classroom or meeting space to have a conversation with the user
- Notebook to capture observations, thoughts, sketches
- Pen
- Time needed for this step: one or more days for the user to take photos; an hour to interview the user and debrief

POTENTIAL OBSTACLES DURING NEED FINDING

Two challenging parts of this phase for design team members can be scheduling times to interview people and then, after an interview or observation, finding the time to capture their thoughts while they are still fresh in their minds.

It can be challenging to see the world through the eyes of someone whose view of life is different from your own. Remain centered on what the users are telling you and keep your own biases and feelings in check.

Read ahead to the next chapter where you will create a character composite of your users. Knowing what features go into an effective character composite that sums up the needs and desires of your users will help team members know what sorts of things they should be asking in their interviews or looking for in their observations. If the team members feel as though they don't have all the information they need to create a character composite, go out and conduct follow-up interviews and observations to fill in knowledge gaps.

For all of the tools presented in this section, you will need to work intentionally to uncover the users' latent needs. The simple things a user does can reveal the most important unmet needs and lead to break-through inspirations. Pay attention to "work-arounds" your users invent or anything they do or say that seems contradictory. I have heard team members who are new to the design process say things like, "I would have modified the questions we are asking earlier in order to develop deeper insights." Don't be hesitant to ask questions of a user or stakeholder that are specific to a situation you're talking about or observing and then following up with "why?" In doing so you will better home in on user needs and be less likely to regret not having the information you need in the synthesis stage.

WHAT'S NEXT?

Having learned three tools to empathize with users and discover their needs, you are prepared to move to the next phase, which is to synthesize your findings. In this phase you and your fellow design team members will immerse yourselves in all that you've discovered in the current phase so as to find the key themes for change, which will ultimately lead to prototyped solutions.

CHAPTER **3**

SYNTHESIS

The members of the Jackson Elementary innovation team were beginning to realize they didn't know their students as well as they wanted to—their users' wants, desires, and, more important, feelings were chiefly unrecognized. In the team meeting where members shared the stories of their interviews, Pete, the fifth-grade teacher, talked about an insight he came to.

"Our students have a lot on their minds besides what they do in our classrooms," he said. "A boy I talked with shared with me that he worries about the balloon in the library and that it if it came loose, it might reach the lights and catch on fire." As Samantha, the fourth-grade teacher, told the story of her conversations with students, she revealed that there was a student who was afraid every day about going to lunch because the cafeteria has so many windows.

"There are so many things like that we don't consider because we haven't had intentional conversations with students about their fears or what makes school feel safe for them."

The Jackson Elementary innovation team gathered in a room to synthesize the findings from their interviews. They had one sheet of paper for each student interview. The sheet contained responses to the interview questions on one side and a summary of highlights and insights from the interviews on the other. The team members took turns telling the story of their interview and what they discovered. As they told their story, the other team members wrote down headlines, quotes, insights, and other highlights from the story onto sticky notes.

Once all the stories had been shared, the team members broke into three groups. Prior to the meeting, the principal, Lori Mills, had placed three sheets of chart paper on the wall, each containing a picture of the face of a Jackson Elementary student. She explained the purpose of the chart paper with the faces.

"Start to categorize your sticky notes as a team and place them in themes on your chart paper. You're not picking out what you think goes with that child. It's important to stay human centered as we work through our findings. I've placed a portrait of a different Jackson Elementary student on each of the sheets of chart paper to serve as a reminder that we're designing for someone else, not ourselves. Therefore, try to focus on what the sticky notes tell you about what our kids are saying they need. Try to come up with a Jackson Elementary profile."

As the team members put their sticky notes into categories, themes began to emerge. One theme had to do with hands-on learning; another related to movement in the classroom. Another focused on homework. Looking across the sheets of chart paper, Samantha said, "We have a ton on movement."

"Yes," Pete concurred, "and on hands-on learning." The rest of the team members agreed.

Sandra said, "I think it's interesting how many students just can't stand the pizza in the cafeteria." As the team discussed prioritizing areas for brainstorming, they concluded that movement needs to be happening in the school. They formed the following "How Might We . . .?" question: How might we get the students at Jackson Elementary moving more in their day?

Now that you have interview and observation data, the time has come to make sense of it all. Chances are you have learned some inspiring things during the need finding phase and you're probably eager to share what you've learned. Your teammates are feeling the same way. By sharing out what each of you have learned in your interviews and observations you're able to derive key insights regarding the nature of the challenge your users face and to set yourself up for a productive brainstorm of solutions (the focus of the next chapter).

There's much that team members tend to find rewarding in this stage. In the need finding and synthesis phases, they start to see the process come together. Reading about the steps is one thing, but now the details are coming into sharper focus. Team members feel as though they are designing something for a real person rather than just generating ideas; the real issues they have been tasked with addressing begin to crystallize. The productive struggle of trying to put themselves in the users' shoes and understand their dilemmas is immensely satisfying for group members.

As the team moves toward synthesis, participants feel as though they are beginning to nail down something concrete. Much of the design process has been theoretical up to this point, but now there's a sense that tangible products will be created. This breathes new life into the process.

The team starts to get to know the users beyond the outward persona of each person. Team members find the opportunity to dig into users' personal stories very interesting and inspiring in ways they don't expect. Some team members feel the most valuable aspect of these phases is the creation of a character composite(s). Even though the composite is semifictional, teams find the character they create is very much a codesigner in the process.

In this chapter I'll brief you on the tools that will take you the furthest fastest. We'll talk about sharing out, character composites, and point-of-view want ads.

SHARE OUT

Sharing out is, in my opinion, one of the most important and rewarding activities in the design cycle. By sharing all the stories each design team member has collected via interviews, shadowing, or photo studies, the team really starts to get in sync. Commonalities are discovered, insights are gained, and many "ahas" are heard. Sharing out is simple, but time consuming. The following steps will help you share and find key themes to help make sense of what you learned in the need finding phase.

Allow about fifteen minutes for each team member to share one user story for each interview or observation they conducted. For instance, if a team member conducted three interviews, one shadow safari, and one user photo study, he or she would share five stories. If team members were paired up on an interview, only one story need be told for that interview (two team members don't have to tell two stories from the same interview). You will need these materials for sharing out:

Materials and Time Needed for Sharing Out

- Notes from all the conversations, observations, and interviews
- Completed conversation and shadow safari worksheets (figures 2.2 and 2.4)
- Sticky notes
- Pens or pencils
- Time needed for this step: About 15 minutes per member per conversation/observation. If three team members conducted two conversations or observations each, budget 60 minutes (10 minutes for each event). If need be, spread it out over a few meetings.

Using their raw notes and the highlights they captured at the end of their interview or observation, each team member tells the story of their user. Listeners should keep track of their ideas using sticky notes, capturing one thought per note and placing it on the table. In addition to the key parts of the story, team members should record quotes, any details they find interesting, barriers the user experiences, and user feelings. This process repeats itself until everyone has told their stories (and hundreds of sticky notes are on the table).

Find Key Themes

Now to make sense of it all. Using a large table, an empty wall, or sheets of blank chart paper, start to move the sticky notes into clusters containing the themes that emerge concerning user desires and needs. What are the key common themes that arise? Write a summary sentence that captures each one. For instance, if the design challenge is centered on the school schedule and one theme among the sticky notes is "electives," then an insightful summary might be (if supported by the notes), "Students want opportunities to pursue electives in addition to core required courses." Or if the design challenge is centered on student use of smartphones at school and one theme among the sticky notes is "anxiety," an insightful summary might be (again, if supported by the notes), "Students don't want to be unable to contact their parents." These themes come into play later when the team develops an empathy map, a tool to envision broad needs across users and a precursor to developing a character composite. Be sure to take photos of your final clustered set of sticky notes, including the theme titles. Check that the picture clearly shows everything written on the notes. You'll refer back to the images when developing an empathy map.

CREATE AN EMPATHY MAP

An empathy map is a visual template widely used by design teams to collect and categorize what a team knows about a set of users.[1] By coalescing traits, feelings, behaviors, and needs across all the users who were part of conversations or observations, teams are better able to come to a shared understanding of user needs.

Figure 3.1 is an example of a standard empathy map. The simple graphic of a human face in the center is intended to drive home the idea that the empathy map is designed to capture what is believed to be inside someone's head. A design team transfers to the map the details they found that tended to cluster together or were the more common from the sharing out step, noting barriers users experience, their feelings, and so forth. This aggregates the details in one place so that a character composite can be created.

Materials and Time Needed for Developing an Empathy Map

- Notes from the sharing out process as well as the themes and the sticky notes that contributed to those themes
- Notes from the need finding events, such as interviews, conversations, or shadow safaris
- Completed conversation and shadow safari worksheets
- A blank empathy map (figure 3.1) for each team member
- Pens or pencils
- Time needed for this step: About 45 minutes

Figure 3.1 Empathy map

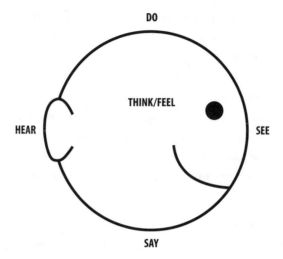

There are two steps in creating an empathy map.

Step 1: Working alone, each design team member pores over the key themes, the sticky notes that contributed to each theme, and their completed conversation and shadow safari worksheets. In revisiting the key themes developed in the sharing out process, each team member begins to jot down on the map the key traits, characteristics, feelings, needs, or desires among the users that align with the following five categories on the map.

- What does the user *see*? What are the users seeing as they experience the challenge that's being explored? Are they seeing their friends do well? Cut class? Skip school? Teachers being helpful? Teachers being dismissive?
- What does the user *hear*? What have the users been hearing in the time leading up to the team's exploration of the challenge—gossip? Rumors? What are people saying to the users? How do they feel about what they are hearing?
- What does the user *say*? What are users saying about the situation at hand? What real quotes do you have from the interviews and observations that are emblematic? Perhaps students say, "I wish

I could use my smartphone during breaks between classes" or "I wish we had more electives in school."

- What does the user *do*? What kind of actions have the users been taking in light of the challenge that's being explored? Are students cutting class to work to support the family? Are they getting a ride to school because the bus feels unsafe?
- What does the user *think* or *feel*? Write down findings from the data showing how users feel about the challenge that's been explored so far. Do they feel good about it? Conflicted? Respected? What matters to them most?

Step 2: Ask a volunteer to serve as recorder for the group and give them a blank empathy map. One at a time, each team member reads out the items they placed on their empathy map. The volunteer recorder writes the items on the new blank map. As the conversation continues the group may begin to see common characteristics, feelings, and behaviors emerge. Similar items may be clustered and given a new name. After all members have had their turn, the group will have a new aggregated empathy map. The team may use this new map as a launch point for developing one or more character composites.

Empathy maps can be powerful tools for informing school change. Jill Thompson, an associate partner at the firm Education Elements and former director of personalized digital learning at Charlotte-Mecklenburg Schools, uses them routinely in her work with educators to make the shift toward more personalized learning. She uses empathy maps to translate the information she gleans from empathetic interviews with students into insights that inform these efforts?[2] For instance, in an interview she may ask:

- What would make you excited to come to school?
- Describe the class you feel most successful in and why.
- How could all teachers help you feel successful?
- Tell me about a time when you learned to do something really difficult. How did you learn it?
- What would your ideal learning experience look like?
- What change do you feel would make the biggest difference in your learning experiences? Why?

After each interview she recasts the responses as key thoughts, feelings, and perceptions the student holds and uses the empathy map as an insight-storage tool. She creates a new empathy map for each interview. On a blank sheet of paper, she draws a circle in the middle and then two intersecting lines to create quadrants. In the first quadrant she writes "Said: What are things this student might say in your class?" In the second quadrant she puts "Thought: What are things this student might be thinking while in your class?" The third quadrant contains "Did: What are some things this student might be doing in the class?" and the last quadrant, "Felt: How might this student feel?" In the center of the circle she writes the student's name and then fills in the quadrants based on the information she learned in her interview. Looking at the empathy maps across students gives Jill insight on the underlying reasons behind student actions, choices, and decisions. This gives teachers greater understanding of students' unmet needs and greater potential to design solutions to challenges in the classroom.

DEVELOP A CHARACTER COMPOSITE

A character composite is a fictional character who embodies the needs, interests, wants, and desires expressed by key segments of your real users. Through the character composite you put a human face on the challenge that stays with the team for the rest of the project. By creating a poster-sized character composite, you are able to have the users in the room with you at all times as the team considers prototype options. It's as if you're able to ask, "Would the elementary-grade students like this solution?" or "Would the parents of our special needs kids appreciate our approach?" and then turn to your character composite to gain insight on the answer.

Materials and Time Needed for Developing a Character Composite
- The empathy map completed by the team
- Character composite worksheet (figure 3.2)
- Character composite mini-poster template (figure 3.3)
- Pens or pencils
- Time needed for this step: About 30 minutes per composite

Figure 3.2 Character composite worksheet

WORKSHEET   SYNTHESIS PHASE

Character Composite

NAME   AGE

Family situation

Hobbies and interests

Media interests

Personal strengths

Personal challenges

Sources of pleasure

Things this person doesn't care for

A habit this person would like to kick

Something under control

Something out of control

Figure 3.3 Character composite mini-poster template

CHARACTER COMPOSITE

Name Here

Portrait Here

| AGE | GRADE | #TAGS | |
| | | #descriptor | #descriptor |

Emblematic Quote Here

| FAVORITE SUBJECTS | FAVORITE BRANDS |

About

Goals

Needs

Doesn't Like

Personality

Creating a character composite involves two steps.

Step 1: Look over the characteristics in the empathy map. What is similar across the users you interviewed and observed? Could one fictional "real" user be created to represent the user in this design challenge? Or do the results from the need finding, once synthesized and embodied in the empathy map, suggest that more than one amalgam character, or user, should be created? Have the design team discuss whether the patterns or similarities in the user characteristics are common enough to warrant creating one overarching character composite, or whether there are smaller but significant segments in the empathy map that justify creating more than one composite. Then use a character composite worksheet to develop one or more characters. For example, if the team were addressing a challenge related to the school schedule in a high school, the design team might arrive at a character composite named Gerardo, whose completed character composite worksheet might look like this:

- Name: Gerardo (or Geraldine)
- Age: 15
- Family situation: adopted with two parents at home
- Hobbies and interests: drawing, sketching, superhero movies, skateboarding
- Media interests: *Good Mythical Morning* on YouTube
- Personal strengths: social, enjoys learning, good sense of humor
- Personal challenges: impulsive, has a hard time sitting still, needs space, doesn't like school very much
- Sources of pleasure: math, drawing, talking with friends
- Things he doesn't care for: crowded hallways, teachers who don't "hear" him
- Habit he wants to kick: not liking school
- Something under control: his room at home
- Something out of control: the choice of classes

Step 2: Use the mini-poster template to draft a character composite. Use additional templates as needed for additional user profiles. Give each character in each character composite a name and a face. Find a portrait image from an online source of copyright-free, royalty-free images, such as compfight.com.

WRITE A POINT-OF-VIEW WANT AD

A final activity in this phase—writing the point-of-view ad—helps you define areas of opportunity.[3] The idea behind a point-of-view want ad is to frame your evolving design challenge into a statement that will set your team up for a productive brainstorm. With this tool you develop a concise summary of what your composite users want. Frame this exercise as though you are your user and you are writing an ad for the personals section of the newspaper or Craigslist. Using the composite above, it's as if you are Gerardo writing a personals ad, except Gerardo is not seeking a date; he's seeking a great school schedule. Here's a guide: Start with a description or some characteristics of your user. Follow that with the word *seeks* and then the thing that will meet their need. End with one or two additional requirements. For example, "Creative, social teenager seeks great school schedule. Interests should include issues of student voice and choice. Willingness to allow me to take electives and have advisory hour a must." A point-of-view want ad focuses the team by keeping certain design constraints in place so when it comes time to prototype, the team is sensitive to things that should or should not be in place.

Recently, I facilitated a workshop for at the European League of Middle Level Educators on applying design thinking to practical challenges in middle school. I enlisted the support of a teacher from the American Overseas School in Rome (AOSR) who agreed to provide the workshop participants with a challenge to address: How might we improve middle-level parent-teacher conferences at the AOSR? Through an empathetic interview, the workshop participants learned that their composite user was a very committed teacher who needed to feel good about parent-teacher conferences. They learned that, at worst, the parent-teacher conferences as they were currently designed, occurring in one big room, felt disruptive, even chaotic. Ultimately, she didn't feel as though the conferences helped the parents, students, or teachers. We crafted a point-of-view ad to capture her feelings and what she ultimately wanted.

Like Gerardo's ad, it mimicked the personals pages, but instead of looking for love, this teacher was looking for a great parent-teacher conference. It went as follows:

> *Energetic Teacher Seeks Awesome Parent-Teacher Conferences*
> Committed, young teacher in an international school seeks awesome parent-teacher conference meetings.
>
> Must be well organized, meet the needs of all parents and teachers, include students as participants in the planning and in the conferences themselves. Think you can make me, my students, and their parents feel proud? Hit me up.
>
> Disruptive? Chaotic? Disorganized? Don't bother.

SYNTHESIS IN ACTION

The synthesis phase can be both exciting and enlightening. Jesse Bacon, principal at Simons Middle School, recalls how transformative this phase was for their innovative team. Team members had completed their interviews and were ready to synthesize their data. They gathered in a room and took turns going through each of the interviews they conducted. As each team member shared the story of their conversation with a student, the others in the room took notes on sticky pads. When all the stories were done, hundreds of sticky notes covered the walls of the room. The team then categorized all the notes and looked for commonalities across the themes. They looked for design opportunities that had two overlapping characteristics: things that the school could accomplish and that the students said they wanted in terms of experience. The work to synthesize the data was a fun experience for the team. What they thought would take an hour and a half turned into a three-hour session—not because the team struggled, but because the sharing of the stories and the connections created across stories was an engaging and illuminating process. What they experienced stood out as yet another example of how the design challenge can shift once user needs are collected, synthesized, and understood. Recall they initially thought there was an opportunity to create a more flexible school schedule so students could go to classes they needed when they needed them, a form of personalized learning. As the team talked and sorted through the sticky notes, new themes came to light. They noticed that they had stopped focusing on the schedule and personalized learning and had begun to talk about physical space. The built environment, the school building, and its relationship to collaborative work kept coming up. They realized they were housed in a 1940s building that was not set up for collaborative work. "The conversation just took us there," Jesse said. "We left scheduling behind and shifted to how we could provide improved collaborative learning spaces.

The themes that emerged as connections told a larger story about what Simons Middle School students needed to have a good learning experience and produce good work:

- Comfortable spaces.
- Inviting colors.
- Areas where students can "just hang out." A traditional chair and desk, or chair and table setup was not desirable.
- Place where we work on projects together.

The school had started to implement project-based learning but had not considered the settings best suited for that work. This is a prime example of how needs gleaned from users can reframe a design challenge. The design team started exploring a challenge that centered on personalized learning, but space and place later took on greater relevance.

Here's an example of how Erin Coyle and the teachers from Fairdale Elementary met to synthesize a body of interview data collected by high schoolers from the neighboring school. They assembled themselves into vertical teams instead of grade-level groups so as to leverage the diversity of an intergrade group. All of the responses from the student conversations had been transcribed onto an online spreadsheet and each vertical team was given a period of time to review all the responses from all the students. Then each vertical team was asked to conduct a deeper dive into the data for a single question on the conversation protocol (i.e., vertical team one synthesized the responses across students for question one, etc.). The teams made notes about the responses to their assigned question and then discussed with the whole group any insights they gleaned from the findings. Based on these insights and their large-group discussion, the vertical teams developed a set of Fairdale student character composites. On chart paper, the teachers drew an image representing a fictional "real" Fairdale student and listed key values, feelings, likes, and dislikes.

When they had considered all the responses and translated their insights into a character composite that represented the values of Fairdale Elementary students, something glaring stood out. Students wanted physical education, something the school once had but did not now have on the schedule. For some time, Fairdale Elementary School had been participating in the district's *compassionate school* initiative. The initiative allowed Fairdale to integrate mindfulness into the day through two compassion classes during the week. In these classes, students learn mindfulness, practice calming techniques, and learn how to be a compassionate citizen. From the teachers' view of the student interview data, the program was working. Data from the interviews told them that their students were happy. They were happy at school, they were happy with their classmates, and they all could say something they liked about school. When this program was put in place, the compassion class took the place of physical education on the schedule. As the teachers shared stories from their findings and crafted the character composites, a contradiction revealed itself. The students were compassionate, they liked being in a compassionate school, they like being compassionate people, and they liked being part of a compassionate community. But they did not like the compassion classes. Nearly every vertical team translated the insights from the interview data into images of students with big hearts, big smiles, and references to a desire for physical education, whether it was a soccer ball, an image of some sport, or just the letters "PE." Erin and the teams formed the following question: How might we maintain the benefits of being a compassionate school without formal compassion classes on the schedule?

CHALLENGES AND ADVICE IN THE SYNTHESIS PHASE

Teams should watch out for challenges like these:

If the list of user needs developed on the character composite seems a bit tame or predictable, this may be a sign the team didn't ask enough "why" questions or questions about the users' lives outside of school. An example of a tame or predictable user want is a fifth grader saying recess is her favorite subject in school. As I noted in chapter 2, let tame or predictable answers be your signal to dive into the five whys to get to the feelings behind the response. If a student says her favorite subject is recess, she may be saying that because it's a critical social time for her, but you'll never know unless you ask. If need be, conduct follow-up interviews or observations with your users to supplement your list of characteristics.

Strive to leave solution making out of this phase—it's not time for that yet. It's natural for educators to problem solve (and to do so as quickly as possible). But trying this too soon can make team members less open-minded to the wide-ranging brainstorms that are coming up in the next phase; running solutions in the back of one's mind makes one less likely to consider other options that could be better. It's best to save the solution-seeking process for the next step, brainstorming.

WHAT'S NEXT?

Having completed the synthesis phase, you and your teammates are ready to embark upon brainstorming. In this phase you'll agree upon, as a team, the pivotal "How Might We . . . ?" question or questions that will drive a productive storm of potential solutions to the challenges posed. You'll then harvest the fruits of the brainstorms to select the ideas best suited to take to prototyping.

CHAPTER **4**

BRAINSTORMING

The innovation team agreed to meet to hold a brainstorming session on the "How Might We . . . ?" question: How might we help the students at Jackson Elementary get more physical activity in their day? In the spirit of codesign, and as a nod to the mind-set of radical collaboration, six students were invited to the brainstorming session. ("Radical" collaboration refers to "non-normal" collaboration, or the inclusion of collaborators who are not normally invited to join you in solving a problem.) It took a few minutes for the students to get used to the fact that they were being treated as equals in the room, but Principal Lori Mills, serving as facilitator, remained outside of the brainstorming circle to act as coach and cheerleader during the session. When she sensed the children (or any participants) were reluctant, or stuck, she would offer an idea to stoke the brainstorm: "How would your parents solve this problem?" or "What would your favorite superhero do to fix this?" In a forty-five-minute session dozens of ideas were generated, some feasible and some silly, but each one was honored and recorded into the brainstorm.

After the brainstorm the team discussed how to harvest the comments so as to narrow the set down to a few plausible ideas. The discussion was fruitful not only for its role in selecting suggestions that might have promise, but also in understanding what the students in the room didn't realize about how schools work. For instance, two of the ideas brainstormed were to have a dance party in class every day and to allow students to run laps in the gym. When these ideas were offered during the brainstorm, they were dutifully recorded and even spurred new thinking. When it came time to harvest the brainstorm, they revisited these suggestions and engaged in a thought experiment regarding the feasibility and desirability of each.

"Design thinking is a mix of having a good idea and taking into account the feasibility and desirability of that idea," Lori said. "So, one thing we have to think about is how our solutions fit in with everything else we've agreed to do."

Deirdre, a fifth grader who joined the brainstorm, said, "So, a dance party might be fun, but we have to find a time to fit it in, right?"

"Yes," said Pete, "and it has to be something that most everyone would like to do. Not everyone likes to dance, right Samantha?"

"Right," agreed Samantha.

"And Jimmy," Lori said to the fourth-grade boy who was in the brainstorm session, "your idea of running laps in the gym is a great thought. I would love for everyone to be able to do that. But we have a gym teacher who has a schedule, and that's her classroom."

Sandra began to think out loud. "You know, we have a way to promote student movement that the school already uses and everyone likes: recess. What if we added a recess?" The team members nodded. Because recess is something everyone understands, from students to teachers to parents, adding one in the day could be something everyone would get behind. They decided to prototype it.

Brainstorming, within the context of design thinking, is the point at which numerous ideas are brought forth as potential solutions to the challenge facing the user. As a general activity, brainstorming has been the target of some derision of late. Authors are quick to point out brainstorming's flaws, including research that brainstorming groups are significantly less productive than nominal groups (people performing on their own with no interaction, whose output is then combined),[1] participants tend to socially loaf (they don't even try to brainstorm), and members fear that their ideas will be blocked or derided.[2]

My criticism of these criticisms is that they take brainstorming out of the context of a design cycle. Most detractors of brainstorming center on its use before any groundwork has been done. The fact is, I'd be loath to engage in a brainstorm that wasn't predicated on the phases discussed in the preceding chapters. Taken out of context, what is the point, really? When were you last asked to suddenly join a group of colleagues to brainstorm ideas to solve a problem without any context or preparation? Not often, I'd imagine. And if you did such a thing, what came of the ideas?

The counterintuitive truth to productive brainstorming is that constraints stoke creativity. Yes, constraining yourselves to a set of parameters that initially don't let you think outside the box actually lets you do just that. Suppose you have a design challenge centered on the school schedule. This already constrains you. Let's say now that the focus of the challenge, based on what you discovered in need finding and synthesis, is to address the unmet needs of student voice and choice in the schedule. You are now constrained even further. But you don't have to go far to *think outside the box* because the box is small.

Brainstorming, in the context of design thinking, has been referred to as "the goal-oriented cousin of daydreaming."[3] It lets you swing for the fences, but with purpose, because the team is about to come up with scores of ideas to solve the unmet needs of important people in your school. This chapter provides tools to help you prepare, conduct, and harvest ideas through the brainstorm.

SET THE TONE

There are two steps to prepare for brainstorming: establishing some ground rules and creating the "How Might We . . . ?" question that serves as the brainstorming prompt. Seven basic rules guide the design thinking process. You can add rules as needed to support your design team.[4] Provide copies of the brainstorming rules below to the team and hang them up in your meeting space for easy referral when you start the process.

CHOOSE A VIABLE "HOW MIGHT WE . . . ?" QUESTION

Before launching a brainstorm session, the team also needs a viable "How Might We . . . ?" question. An example of a "How Might We . . . ?"

Rules for Brainstorming

- **GO FOR QUANTITY.** At this stage, brainstorming is a numbers game. You want a lot of ideas, not necessarily a lot of good ideas. In workshops I conduct, I set an aspirational (and admittedly difficult) challenge for teams to generate fifty ideas in six minutes, during which many come up with thirty or more ideas. It's reasonable for a team to generate a hundred ideas in an hour.
- **BUILD ON THE IDEAS OF OTHERS.** Leverage the time-tested tool of the improvisational actor by saying "Yes, and . . . " after hearing another person's idea. Ideas offered at this point are not only possible solutions but also jumping-off points to new solutions.
- **ENCOURAGE WILD IDEAS.** Wild ideas that will never work can often lead to a subsequent idea that turns out to be the gem you were looking for. I usually say to my students and workshop participants, "Your ideas do not have to obey the laws of physics, just the laws of [insert your local jurisdiction here]."
- **DEFER JUDGMENT.** The key to a brainstorm that engenders teamwork, optimism, good feelings, and new ideas is to allow everyone to feel as though they can say anything on their mind without fear of judgment. Therefore I encourage teams not to block ideas or make judgmental comments like, "Oh, that'll never work."
- **KEEP IT TO ONE CONVERSATION AT A TIME.** It's hard to build on ideas if you can't hear them. Be sure everyone is paying attention to whoever is talking. An oral brainstorm can get a bit noisy and it can be easy to talk over one another. When that happens, it's difficult for the scribe to capture everything that's being said.
- **STAY ON THE TOPIC.** The mission in the brainstorm is to come up with a lot of ideas for the topic at hand. By not staying on topic you risk missing out on potential solutions, and fall into generating ideas for a completely different issue.
- **WHEN IT SUITS YOU, DRAW IT.** Sometimes making a quick sketch on a sticky note can convey much more than words.

question is "How might we enhance families' sense of belonging at school?"

To create a "How Might We . . . ?" question, there are just three steps: revisit the challenge, test each question for viability, and then determine who should participate. Here's what you need to have on hand:

Materials and Time Needed to Choose a "How Might We . . . ?" Question

- Character composite(s) the team created (figure 3.2)
- Point-of-view ad created earlier
- Time needed for this step: 20 minutes

The first step is to revisit the challenge (see figure 1.4) and, using the worksheet in figure 4.1, turn insights into "How Might We . . . ?" questions for consideration. Recall in chapter 3, when we were talking about "How Might We . . . ?" questions? They come in handy again here. Back then, we were setting up the general challenge. How has your challenge shifted or been modified since that time? It could be more specific now or might have taken a left turn into an urgent area that came about from an insight your team had. We now turn to the "How Might We . . . ?" questions again as a tool to launch a brainstorm.

Let's say your team initially decided to tackle a challenge related to the school's schedule. Consider everything you have learned about your users through interviews and observations, all the insights you derived from synthesizing the data, and gaze into your character composite's eyes to refresh your mind of what the salient unmet needs and desired emotions are for your user. What needs solving? This is where the character composite comes in handy. Recall that the character composite represents a fictional "real" person, representing the most salient characteristics of an array of users the team interviewed and observed. Use the character composite to have a team conversation about insights or "ahas" the members notice about the person portrayed in the composite. Do the same thing with the point-of-view want ad. Then have a team discussion, listing as many insights as you can make about your user. Insights are revealing things you have discovered about your user. Think of them as the big "ahas." Write them down. Now, taking the list, try rephrasing each as a "How Might We . . . ?" question. Your goal is to find opportunities for design, so if your insights suggest several "How Might We . . . ?" questions, that's great. Write down as many questions as your team can muster.

At the European League of Middle Level Educators workshop I mentioned in chapter 3, we used the point-of-view want ad to craft a set of "How Might We . . . ?" questions from which a brainstorm could be launched. The workshop participants came up with eleven candidate "How Might We . . . ?" questions to focus a brainstorm. They were:

How Might We . . . ?
1. involve students in quality ways?

2. make the teachers feel better about the conferences?
3. make teachers prepare more for conferences?
4. make the teachers feel proud of their conferences?
5. ensure that the students are the focal point?
6. make the experience enjoyable?
7. determine whether we reached our goals?
8. make time for all the steps?
9. help students understand their strengths and weaknesses?
10. do conferences in alternative formats?
11. better schedule the conferences ahead of time?

The workshop participants discussed the pros and cons of each question, keeping in mind the composite teacher for whom they were designing solutions. Ultimately, they chose a new, modified question that captured what needed solving: How might we create alternative formats for parent conferences?

Next, test each "How Might We . . . ?" question for viability. Your "How Might We . . . ?" question is the launchpad for your brainstorm session. Therefore it should be the one question that is focused on meeting the needs of your user and will generate a large number of possible answers. As you draft candidate questions, here are a couple of ways to test their quality.

Ask yourself if each one allows for a variety of solutions. If it doesn't, broaden it. Here's an example of a "How Might We . . . ?" question that's too broad: "How might we improve education?" With a question like that, you will never create any actionable solutions in your brainstorm.

Here's a question that's too narrow: "How might we design a new training that is delivered on iPads and addresses outcome 3.2.1 of our math standards?" In that example, you've embedded the solution to the problem in the question; you presume the solution to whatever problem you have is training delivered on iPads. That really restricts a brainstorm.

Using dot voting (see chapter 1, "Choose One Challenge"), decide on the one question to brainstorm by ensuring it strikes the right balance between too broad and too narrow, doesn't have solutions embedded in the question, and contains the name of the user (you can use the name of

Figure 4.1 Choosing a viable "How Might We...?" question

WORKSHEET   BRAINSTORMING PHASE

Turning Insights into "How Might We...?" Questions

CHARACTER COMPOSITE USER NAME

Insight or "aha!" about the user   **How might we...**

Example: Angela is far more shy than   Example: ...better differentiate en-
her teachers realize.   gagement opportunities for students
                                               like Angela?

SELECT ONE QUESTION FROM ABOVE FOR BRAINSTORMING; MODIFY FOR VIABILITY AS NEEDED

How might we...

Viability check

☐ Does not presume a solution   ☐ Allows for a variety of solutions   ☐ Not too broad the person in your character composite) in the question. For instance, if your user is a teenager named Sarah and her challenge is healthier eating, these are some possible questions:[5]

- How might we make healthy eating appealing to Sarah?
- How might we inspire Sarah to choose healthier eating options?
- How might we make healthy eating something to which Sarah aspires?
- How might we make nutritious food more affordable for Sarah?

The final step is to determine who should participate in the brainstorm. The team should invite outsiders to join the session. They could be users (students), partners, or other stakeholders who have an interest in the challenge. Approximately ten people is a good size for the group.

CONDUCT A BRAINSTORM

You are now ready to conduct a brainstorm. Here's what you'll need.

Materials and Time Needed to Conduct a Brainstorm
- The final "How Might We . . . ?" question (from the worksheet in figure 4.1)
- Character composites
- Brainstorming rules (listed earlier in this chapter)
- Sticky notes
- Whiteboard or poster paper
- Markers
- A volunteer to capture the brainstorm on the whiteboard or poster paper
- A facilitator to keep the brainstorm going
- Time needed for this step: About an hour. For setup and briefing the team: 10 to 15 minutes. The brainstorm can take 10 to 30 minutes depending on the question, group dynamic, ideas generated, and so on.

Ensure that the "How Might We . . . ?" question is prominently displayed for everyone to see. Elect a person from the group to be the scribe, capturing the storm on paper or a whiteboard. The advantage of using a whiteboard is that everyone can see the list of ideas grow, and what's on the board can inspire new ideas. An initial time of fifteen minutes is good, and the team can use some of the techniques below to stoke the brainstorm in subsequent ten- to fifteen-minute chunks. Some other things to keep in mind:[6]

- Select a space to hold the brainstorm where everyone has some elbow room but still feels like they are part of the group.
- Hand out sticky notes and pens to everyone in case ideas come too fast for the scribe to handle. Participants can add these to the whiteboard.
- Consider setting up the space so no one is more than two steps from the whiteboard and can add their idea should the mood strike them.
- Display the character composite where everyone can see it.

Start Brainstorming

To start the brainstorm, check that everyone on the team is ready to begin. Make sure everyone can see, or has a copy of, the brainstorming rules. Confirm that everyone is clear on the "How Might We . . . ??" question and has paper, sticky notes, and a pen. Ask if the scribe is ready. Once everyone feels prepared, the facilitator says, "Begin!" The group starts brainstorming, doing their best to adhere to the rules listed at the start of the chapter. The facilitator can help the brainstorm stay productive by chiming in as necessary with a rule reminder (e.g., "Let's build on that. How could we say 'Yes, and . . . ' to that?") to tossing in a stoking strategy to revive stalled thinking (e.g., "How would your significant other solve this question?")

Teaching Students to Brainstorm

Catlin Tucker is a teacher in Sonoma County, California, who has used brainstorming with her students as a way to involve them in generating ideas that will drive class projects.[7] After having an opportunity to see the way a team at IDEO conducted a brainstorm, Catlin and her teaching team elected to develop a protocol for how their students should conduct brainstorms. It's a hybrid of individual and group work, which affords participants a chance to think on their own and out loud. Here's her approach:

Step 1: Silent three-minute brainstorm using sticky notes. Students have three minutes to silently generate as many ideas as possible, writing one idea per sticky note. She emphasizes to her students that there are no bad ideas because even off-the-wall ideas can spark others worth considering.

Step 2: Take turns sharing ideas. Students take turns reading the ideas written on each sticky note and adding them to a whiteboard or other surface the group can see. Catlin has the students listen without judgment, asking that their questions and comments be saved for the next step.

Step 3: Categorize and discuss. Once all students have had a chance to share their sticky notes and post them on the board, they then group the stickies that have common themes. As they do so they are invited to ask questions about any idea in the brainstorm thus far—be it to clarify, understand, or build upon. Students are encouraged to offer new ideas or add to ones already posted.

Step 4: Identify the most interesting ideas. Once all of the sticky notes are posted and categorized, each member of the group is given five sticky dots to place on their favorite ideas. Visually, this creates a form of a heat map, highlighting the ideas or categories that are the most interesting to the group.

Step 5: Document the brainstorm. Catlin asks students to take photos of the brainstorm to capture the results. Because her students maintain a digital notebook, they can file the photo for future reference.

Catlin's ability to build creative capacity in her students gives credence to their voice, helping them know they are heard and better preparing them to codesign with others in their school.

Stoking a Brainstorm

There may be times when a lull overcomes the brainstorm. If this happens, try these tips to keep the brainstorm going.[8]

- Add "What if" constraints to the brainstorm that restrict the technology, timing, space, size, or people who make or use the solutions. This forces the team to consider new features or ideas so that they will work inside the new constraint. For example: "What if we could only use technology available in the 1800s?" "What if our solutions can only be used before 8:00 a.m.?" "What if our solutions had to be used only in a car?" "What if what we make must fit in a child's hand?" or "What if it can only be used by the lunch team?"
- Add a time constraint to the brainstorm, such as challenging the group to develop fifty ideas in fifteen minutes.
- Add conceptual constraints to the brainstorm, such as "How would the Avengers do this?" (or "your significant other," or "Amazon," or come up with your own actor). Or "How could this be solved without any technology?" "What if students were in charge?" "How could this issue take advantage of parents?"
- Play the opposite game.[9] If the goal is to come up with ways to encourage greater family involvement at school, brainstorm ways to get families to *avoid* being involved with school. Discuss the insights from such a list and flip them into possible solutions. See my example below of how we made this work in an elementary school.
- Hold a contest by dividing the brainstormers into two or three teams and offer a prize to the group that comes up with the most ideas in an allotted amount of time.
- Any of the above can be mixed and matched. For instance, use a variant "How Might We . . . ?" question with a time constraint.

Stoking a Brainstorm by Turning Bad Ideas into Good

The primary school at the International School of Ho Chi Minh City (ISHCMC) is an early education (age two) through grade 5 (EE2-5) International Baccalaureate school in Vietnam. My colleague Beth Rous and I combined three steps of brainstorming, prototyping, and feedback into a compressed time frame to jumpstart ideas for how teachers and leaders at the school could create continuity across grades. Rather than ask teachers to brainstorm ways to improve continuity of curriculum, collaboration, and learning across grades, we had them do the opposite: brainstorm the worst ideas possible. In step one, teachers and leaders from across the school broke into teams of about ten people each. One team member was assigned to be a timekeeper, and another the team's scribe. The timekeeper set a timer for five minutes. Before beginning, the teams were given the following instructions: "Take five minutes to brainstorm the worst ideas you can think of. You can use the following prompts:"

- What are ways we can isolate our grades and teachers more?
- How can we keep good ideas from being shared across people or places in our school?
- What are some terrible taglines for a campaign to keep teachers isolated?

We gave them a handout with guidelines to help each team come up with a lot of bad ideas. On it they were encouraged to come up with wild ideas that, in turn, can give rise to creative leaps; build on the ideas of others; stay focused on their original prompt; allow one person at a time to speak; and go for lots and lots of ideas.

In the end there was no shortage of bad ideas from the brainstorm, some hilariously cringeworthy. Here are just a few that the teams came up with:

- Talking to other teachers is forbidden.
- Block off corridors to non-grade-level teachers.
- Document nothing.
- Dictate to teachers in grades below what they should be teaching.
- Reward hoarding of resources.
- Send postcards to teachers in other grades with negative feedback about their work.
- Ensure planning periods prevent collaboration with other teachers.

After the brainstorming phase concluded, we asked the teams to take ten minutes to turn one of their bad ideas into a good idea. We asked the teams to pick one of the ideas generated in the brainstorm that they could flip into a great idea with a little work. We then asked them to give their idea a name and sketch it on a sheet of chart paper using markers or any other materials they wished (paint, stickers, other media). We did constrain them to only drawing, forbidding the use of words on their chart except for labels to call out parts of their drawing. We did this because we were more interested in their ideas visually and wanted to curtail any desire to create a prototype that resembled a bulleted presentation slide.

Finally, the teams gathered in a common space with the chart paper containing their ideas. Each team had a representative describe their bad idea, how it was flipped into a good idea, and what problem it would solve. All the participants in the room were allowed to use three sticky notes on which to write their feedback: one for "I like . . . " one for "I wish . . . ," and one for "I wonder . . . ." They then placed the notes on the prototype.

What were some of the new "good" ideas that emanated from the mass of awfulness?

- A communal, connected common space for teachers, students, and families across all grades to gather.
- The use of rivers and bridges as metaphors for how space, time, and technology could be used to increase cross-grade sharing among teachers.
- Student pairing, or even broader mixing of grade levels on a daily basis.
- The development of a new position whose sole job is to connect grades from primary to secondary.
- Ways for the school community to disconnect from technology so as to better connect with each other.

Improving cross-grade collaboration and continuity had been a topic within ISHCMC that felt important to address but no time could be found to kickstart a productive, cross-class conversation on solving it. This exercise took about one hour. By combining a bad-idea brainstorm with rapid prototyping and feedback, the team at ISHCMC developed a platform for discussing what kinds of pilot initiatives they could try.

A Variation on Brainstorming: Brainwriting

Brainwriting is a written alternative to the verbal brainstorming approach discussed above.[10] Instead of having team members say their ideas out loud, you ask them to write down their answers to a "How Might We . . . ?" question on paper or a card. After a few minutes you ask the participants to pass their paper or card to another person who then reads the ideas and adds new ones. This process repeats until everyone has their original sheet or card back. One way to systematically run a brainwriting session is using the 6-3-5 method, where six people write down three ideas in five minutes. At the end of the thirty-minute brainwriting session there is the potential for $6 \times 3 \times 6$ (6 people $\times$ 3 ideas $\times$ 6 rounds), or 108 ideas. Because these are timebound sessions (no more than thirty minutes of brainwriting) and don't require many people or a facilitator, they are fairly easy to run; set up as many as you need if you want to include specialized groups, such as one just with parents or just with teachers. Here is how you run a 6-3-5 brainwriting session.[11]

Materials and Time Needed for a 6-3-5 Brainwriting Session

- "How Might We . . . ?" question (from figure 4.1, the Turning Insights into "How Might We . . . ?" Questions worksheet)
- Character composites
- A 6-3-5 brainwriting template (figure 4.2)
- Time needed for this step: About 45 minutes. For setup and briefing the team: 5 minutes; for the brainwriting: 30 minutes; for postbrainwriting discussion: 10 minutes.

Step 1: Gather six people to participate in the 6-3-5 session.

Step 2: Distribute one copy of the 6-3-5 brainwriting template with the names of the participants already filled in the leftmost column.

Step 3: Display the "How Might We . . . ?" question prominently for the participants.

Step 4: Each participant writes down three ideas within five minutes on the row of the sheet next to their name.

Step 5: After five minutes are up, the sheet is passed to the next participant. The clock is reset for five minutes and the

Figure 4.2 6-3-5 Brainwriting template

	1	2	3
Participant 1 Name			
Participant 2 Name			
Participant 3 Name			
Participant 4 Name			
Participant 5 Name			
Participant 6 Name			

participants write down three new ideas, this time with the benefit of being able to see, and hopefully build upon, the ideas written by the previous participant.

Step 6: The process repeats itself until each of the six participants has developed three ideas on each sheet.

The advantages of the 6-3-5 method are that it's easy to use, it doesn't require a moderator, and all participants are active and involved in the brainstorm process, which doesn't always occur in an oral brainstorming. It is also an advantage to be able to identify the author in case an idea warrants follow-up or clarification. A couple of disadvantages should be pointed out. Some participants may have a hard time describing their ideas concisely in the small space provided in the template. This can be mitigated by encouraging participants to describe their ideas in headline format. Also, some participants may also feel pressured by the time constraint. Let participants know the 6-3-5 brainwriting is not a test and they are not required to complete three ideas per round. And there is no penalty for coming back to a sheet and filling out additional ideas if a participant thinks of more than three.

It's suggested that this approach can reduce any anxiety that some members may have and keeps cross talk down if the group you have invited to brainstorm has become too big. One interesting affordance of brainwriting is there's no practical limit on the number of people who can participate in the process. Imagine freeing yourself from the 6-3-5 method and convening a hundred people in a room, each of whom is handed an index card with a "How Might We . . . ?" question printed on it. Each person could write an idea related to the question on the card and pass it to the left. Complete this cycle three times and you have up to three hundred new answers to the question.

HARVEST THE BRAINSTORM

The last activity in this phase is harvesting the brainstorm. At the end of the brainstorm you should be left with scores of potential ideas for prototyping, some of which are outrageous, or even silly, and some that are very viable.

Materials and Time Needed for Harvesting the Brainstorm

- "How Might We . . . ?" question (from figure 4.1)
- Character composite
- Whiteboard
- Sticky notes
- Colored adhesive dots (one color is fine)
- Markers
- Time needed for this step: 15 to 20 minutes

How do you go about culling the set of ideas down to a few that are good candidates for prototyping? I'm partial to two tools.

The first tool, dot voting, works well here (I described this tool in chapter 1 on choosing a challenge). If not already on display, transcribe all the brainstorm ideas onto a whiteboard or chart paper. Hand out sheets of sticky dots to the team members. Ask each person to place one to three dots next to the solutions they would like the team to work on. No team member may place more than three dots on any solution. The solution with the most dots is selected for prototyping.

The second tool is called the four categories method (see figure 4.3), which is one of my favorites because it allows you to select plausible solutions and keep some far-fetched but potentially effective ideas in the wings.[12] In this method the team selects one idea for each of the following four categories:

1. The rational choice
2. The idea most likely to delight the user
3. The team's favorite
4. The long shot

When I work with preK–12 schools in which we have students, teachers, and school leaders in the room, I describe the long shot as follows: "This is the solution that you believe your principal will never, ever, ever let you do, but if he or she did, it would be awesome." You would be shocked at how often reasonable, viable ideas get put in this category by students.

From these four ideas the team selects one to take forward to the prototyping stage. This can be done via acclimating through discussion, or via dot voting.

Figure 4.3 Four categories method for selecting ideas to prototype

WORKSHEET   BRAINSTORMING PHASE

Four Categories (Harvesting a Brainstorm)

The rational choice

The idea most likely to delight the user

The team's favorite

The long shot

CHALLENGES AND ADVICE IN BRAINSTORMING

Provide context and goals for the brainstorming session well before the meeting. For instance, two days before the meeting, provide advance reading material or contextual information about the design challenge up to this point. Give everyone an idea of what an ideal outcome for the meeting will be (e.g., "We want to come up with fifty ideas that address our challenge"). All of this helps team members arrive feeling prepared.[13]

It's okay to ask the team members to "pre-brainstorm." When sending out the advance material, ask recipients to start thinking about possible solutions to the challenge.[14]

Use a "suggestion box" approach to capture anonymous ideas after the brainstorming session has ended. People always come up with ideas after the fact, and often there are participants who are too shy to share in the meeting. An electronic suggestion box can be set up using Google Forms, for instance.[15]

Consider brainwriting if you are concerned that with the open brainstorm format, the composition of the group may privilege ideas from dominant team members.

While building off others' ideas is a technique for coming up with new ones, for this to really work, all team members must pay attention to the suggestions offered in the brainstorm. Researchers in a laboratory setting have increased brainstorm productivity by improving the group's attention to one another's ideas by telling participants that their memory of the suggestions would be tested.[16] As a practical matter, it may not be feasible to test participants' recall of the ideas created in a brainstorm (their disdain for being quizzed notwithstanding). However, a facilitator could encourage individuals to pay more attention to group members' ideas.

WHAT'S NEXT?

In this chapter we covered the steps needed to complete a brainstorm. This sets the stage for prototyping. In prototyping, I'll show you how to take the ideas you came up with here and make them real. Further, you'll get a chance to test those ideas with users and then use their feedback to make the solutions you've developed even better.

CHAPTER 5

PROTOTYPING

Principal Lori Mills accepted the mandate from the innovation team that Jackson Elementary should prototype the idea of adding an additional recess to the day. As it stood now, there was one recess, in the afternoon. Because implementing a new recess involved issues of scheduling, staffing, and physical exercise, Lori assembled a pilot testing team of teachers, office staff, fellow administrators, and the PE teacher in addition to the innovation team. The new team turned out to be instrumental in not only supporting the pilot concept, but also helping identify potential roadblocks.

"We have an issue," Lori said to some teachers on the innovation team, after her first meeting with the pilot testing team. "While I'm excited about seeing how an additional recess will help our students, it's not as simple as we thought. State regulations say we can't just add a recess without taking into account the instructional time it takes away."

"Well, how can we make sure every kid in our school is getting movement more than one time a day?" asked Samantha, the fourth-grade teacher.

Lori thought for a moment. "Let's keep this curricular at first so we're not accused of losing instructional minutes. We don't want someone to come in and say, 'This is not okay, you're losing instructional minutes.' So, how could we prototype this so our kiddos get the movement they need, and we can prove they are still receiving instruction while they're engaged in physical activity?"

The team decided to use a hybrid of an experiential prototype and a "fake it" prototype to test their idea. They planned to have the kids experience new opportunities for movement during the day through fake recesses that still had instructional components. The first thing they did was call the time something besides recess. They called it morning movement, a label they thought wasn't likely to raise any eyebrows in the district or state. Then Samantha came up with a way to integrate it into the curriculum for her fourth graders. Students would pass a ball back and forth during a unit on social studies, or practice multiplication facts in a game that involved running outside. No matter what, children did not miss instruction during morning movement.

The team members weren't trying to cheat the system, but rather be strategic about how they could determine the viability of this concept and still make sure it was instructional. There was a moment, however, when they thought what they were prototyping would be disapproved of at the state level.

As a part of a formative state department of education program review that Lori had submitted some months prior, Jackson Elementary had highlighted that the school was building more movement into the day for its students. Samantha felt a lump in her throat when she was asked to come to a school conference room to join a video conference with a state department of education officer—they wanted to hear more about "morning movement." Samantha thought to herself, "Oh, no. We're going to get in trouble for inserting this extra movement time." But when she got to the conference room, she found out it was the complete opposite. The state officer was very interested in how Jackson Elementary was able to provide students more opportunities to move during the day. The officer even asked if she could send a team of people out to Jackson to highlight what they were doing.

Prototyping sounds complex, but it need not be. In fact, I want to argue here that prototyping should be the opposite. It should be rapid and low cost if it's to be relevant and useful. We prototype to learn; thus, we invest only the time and resources needed to determine what works (and, more important, what doesn't work) before making expensive bets on solutions.

This rapid, low-cost approach is best illustrated by a popular orientation exercise used in design thinking circles known as the "Wallet Project." It was developed at the Hasso Plattner Institute for Design at Stanford, better known as the dSchool. The exercise is designed to take novices through the steps of an entire design thinking cycle in about ninety minutes. In one step in the exercise, participants are asked to brainstorm five solutions to a challenge their partner is facing, but they must draw each solution inside a two- by three-inch rectangle, of which five are arrayed across a page. Upon hearing this, many participants audibly groan. For some reason people are physically and emotionally reluctant to portray any idea, even simple ones, visually. They would rather turn each of the little boxes into tiny presentation slides with bullets followed by sentences describing their idea to their partner. When I run the exercise, I assure everyone at this point that they need not be great artists to complete this step—that stick figures, boxes, circles, arrows, and so on are fine, but they must draw.

What happens next is remarkable. In spite of all the gnashing of teeth, participants make sets of very simple drawings that, in the end, impart much more information about their ideas than any multipage memo could convey. To be sure, aesthetically speaking, most of the sketches are awful. Yet they are beautiful in so many other ways. The participants are able to point to key aspects of the idea, trace with their finger how a process would evolve, show ideas in succession like a film strip. And their partners are able to do likewise. They can point to parts of the drawing to ask questions, or even take up a pen and add a little part to the drawing as a potential improvement. I ask participants after the exercise concludes what they took away from the experience, and invariably we discuss how working visually, even in the most rudimentary ways, helps convey ideas more clearly than verbal descriptions. It invites reaction, conversation, and collaboration. And, most important, when participants showed their sketches to their partners, they learned more about their partner's needs. Need finding, as noted earlier, never really ends.

There are three chief reasons why you should prototype.[1] First, the act of building or making something is a way to think. Being able to see and interact with an idea allows you to think about the viability of your solution in new ways. Second, it's the principal way you obtain feedback from users and other stakeholders. Third, it's a fast and cheap way to find out what doesn't work so you can concentrate on what does work. In other words, it lets you fail fast to succeed sooner.

PREPARING TO PROTOTYPE: ANTICIPATING FEEDBACK

We prototype to think. By creating a prototype of a solution you seek to make it real. And in doing so you invariably think about how your solution will work in the world and how your users will interact with it. This, in turn, implies you will need to solicit feedback from your target users. So it's worth thinking a bit about what that will feel like and how you will do it. First let's talk about how you should *think* about your prototype. The team has put a great deal of time into the challenge up to this point and it's reasonable to expect the participants to be a bit proud of their solutions. Well, I have to tell you something. Those ideas you have come up with, the few that have risen to the top among hundreds, and which were born out of a labor of data collection, synthesis, thought, and care, are not precious.

Let me repeat that. Your ideas are not precious.

Remember, prototypes are strong opinions weakly held. So, while your ideas are not precious, the feedback you are about to obtain is gold. Because in the end, prototyping is just fancy need finding. And that's what this process is all about—finding unmet needs and meeting them.

"That's fine, John," you say. "But what do I do when our ideas are criticized?" Good question, and a fair one at that. One of the reasons people tend not to welcome feedback is because they are afraid to hear criticism. Once you are able to internalize that your ideas are not precious and your goal is to better understand the user, then all feedback, good and bad, is useful because it contributes to something that will make your users' lives better.

So, as you go through the steps described below in obtaining feedback on your prototypes, keep the following tips in mind.

- Present your prototype in a neutral manner so that you don't indicate you favor or disfavor it in any way.
- Don't defend your prototype.
- Revel in any instance where a user misuses your prototype. When this happens, it means at least one of two things: you missed a crucial feature in the prototype, or you just discovered something that will make the solution even better.
- After any comment from a user, reply only with "Thank you." I learned this from Rolf Faste, Bernie Roth, and Doug Wilde when I worked at Stanford University. "Thank you" means "I heard it, I caught it, and if I choose to do something with that later, I will."
- If you have a little bit of time before or after conducting formal feedback rounds, you can obtain quick, valuable feedback on any prototype using "Like, wish, wonder."
  - Ask the person taking in your solution to say something they like about your solution by starting with the words *I like*. For instance, "I like how you considered the voices of students in your solution."
  - Then ask the person to say something they wish were different about the idea by starting with the words *I wish*. For example, "I wish the design took student voices into account."
  - Then let them offer something that's on their mind or that they wonder about by starting with the words *I wonder*. For instance, "I wonder if this would work in a kindergarten classroom."
  - Reply after each of these with "Thank you."

There are three types of prototype that I recommend teams use: storyboard, experiential, and "fake it" prototypes that are designed to portray complex or potentially expensive solutions in simple ways. Which one of these you pick depends on how much you want to know about the intricacies of your solution and the questions you want to answer. If you are seeking overarching conceptual feedback on a solution, or looking to ascertain how people may feel or react to an idea, a storyboard may do the trick. But if the questions you seek answers to are predicated on having users interact with a solution, then an experiential or "fake it" prototype may suit your needs better. One thing all three of these proto-typing approaches have in common is that they are designed to be rough and rapid. By working with a fast and simple process, you can be more confident of a success because the investment in time and resources can remain very low yet produce a great deal of valuable feedback.

STORYBOARD PROTOTYPES

A storyboard is a sequence of drawings typically accompanied by a brief description of a scene or some dialogue between characters in the sto-ryboard. While storyboards are a staple of the entertainment industry, used to represent the shots planned for a movie or television program, they are also a simple yet powerful way to prototype a solution. In their finished form storyboards often resemble a comic book.

Storyboard prototypes are useful when you want to portray the con-text for a solution and how those who will experience the solution will then act and feel. For instance, if the design team were pursuing solu-tions to improve the school schedule, and the solutions were centered on introducing electives into the high school schedule, the team could develop a storyboard depicting a user's journey through her school day. It could show her entering the school, attending classes, engaging in activities that spark her interest in an elective topic, and being disap-pointed in discovering electives are scant offerings at her school; then it could turn to a depiction of how a series of electives is offered, how she fits the electives into her schedule, and how by taking the electives she is able to reach a key goal. There are three steps for creating a storyboard: create a story, put it to paper, and bring it to life. Here's what you'll need.

Materials and Time Needed for Storyboarding
- Notes from all the conversations, observations, and interviews
- Brainstorm harvest from dot voting or the four categories worksheet
- Completed conversation and shadow safari worksheets
- Sticky notes
- Pens or pencils
- Time needed for this step: 30 minutes to one hour

The first step in the process is creating the story. Storyboards should have a bit of a dramatic arc to them (they contain the word *story*, after all). They should depict what the situation is for users prior to the proposed solution and how the users feel at that stage. Then the story should introduce the solution and describe one or two subsequent behaviors or feelings held by the users thanks to their interaction with the solution. The story should end with a final positive (and expected) result for the users.

There's a formula for this called the Story Spine Game (see figure 5.1), which you can play in your team.[2] Go around in a circle and improvise the development of a story that will go into a storyboard. Start with "once upon a time" and have one person at a time spontaneously fill in the blank for each line in the worksheet until you have reached the end of the story. This is a good way to collectively envision how your solution will look in the real world.

The second step in the process is to get some sketches on paper. Using the outline you developed using the story spine worksheet, draft a simple storyboard (see figure 5.2).

If you don't have a template, you can easily make one: Take an 8.5-× 11-inch sheet of paper. Fold it in half four times; then unfold it to reveal eight panels. Use one or more panels to portray each step in the story. Don't get hung up on drawing abilities. This is about your idea, not artistic skill. There are resources on the internet you can turn to for developing a storyboard. These include online tools such as Storyboard That and Scenes.[3] The final step in the process, which is optional, is to bring your storyboard to life. You can do this by turning your paper prototype into a skit prototype, in which a group of people act out the experience portrayed in the storyboard in front of a group of users, partners, or stakeholders. My colleague Dan Gilbert and I once led a design thinking workshop for school leaders in Iowa in which they crafted prototype solutions to address the challenge of improving professional learning communities in schools. One group of participants, composed of associate superintendents, directors of instruction, and the like, acted out their story in a puppet show using puppets fashioned out of brown paper lunch sacks decorated with markers. In their puppet show, they portrayed what a professional learning community in a school district

Figure 5.1 Story spine game

WORKSHEET   PROTOTYPING PHASE

Story Spine

A story about (user name)

Once upon a time...

Every day...

Until one day...

Because of that...

Because of that...

Because of that...

Until finally...

And ever since then...

The moral of the story is...

Figure 5.2 Storyboard template

WORKSHEET   PROTOTYPING PHASE

Storyboard Template

❶

CAPTION/DESCRIPTION

❷

CAPTION/DESCRIPTION

❸

CAPTION/DESCRIPTION

❹

CAPTION/DESCRIPTION

❺

CAPTION/DESCRIPTION

❻

CAPTION/DESCRIPTION

❼

CAPTION/DESCRIPTION

❽

CAPTION/DESCRIPTION

would look like for teachers and leaders who were seeking solutions to improving professional dialogue.

Feedback on Storyboard Prototypes

For storyboard prototypes, design teams can use a feedback protocol like the one described below. Ask one to three users to meet with you. These can be persons who were part of the need finding process or new users who fit the profile of the character composite you developed. These are the general steps:

1. Explain what's going on.
2. Show the storyboard prototype.
3. Capture the feedback.

Explain What's Going On

Say the following in your own words to the persons providing feedback:

> Let me tell you a bit about the needs we discovered and what we're trying to address.
>
> - We want to *[describe the design challenge in one sentence]*.
> - Our question is "How might we *[insert your 'How Might We' question here]*?"
> - We discovered the following unmet needs:
>   - [List a few of the key unmet needs or insights that drove the prototype development.]
> - In our time together, I'd like to:
>   - Give you a tour of our prototype and get your reactions.
>   - Ask you to rank some other solutions we see.
>
> Ready to begin?

After the users have toured or experienced the prototype, ask questions like this, always following up with "why?":

- What should we keep in here? What do you like?
- What should we increase? Should there be more of anything?
- What should we get rid of?
- What, in this solution, meets *[describe an unmet need]* and what does not?

- What information have we missed in all this?
- Is this just for *[user category; e.g., parents]* or is it for *[a different user category; e.g., teachers]* as well?

Storyboarding can be used effectively to solicit feedback on potential solutions from large groups. Members of design teams in school districts of the Uplands region of Indiana chose to use storyboarding as they applied design thinking to reimagine how their preK–12 curricula could be better aligned to their communities' educational and workforce needs. Their work crossed stakeholder boundaries within their communities and involved need finding interviews with students, teachers, parents, and local industry members to arrive at a user-driven sense of what their community needed. Because their work would ultimately lead to large-scale investment and change within their districts, being able to present prototype ideas to their community members took on an outsized importance. Community-wide investment is expensive, so implementing solutions that weren't right could lead to costly, ineffective initiatives. At the same time, knowing which solutions, among several, would resonate most with stakeholders was hard to predict. The school districts, as well as the foundation underwriting their design work, thought storyboarding would be a good component of an idea refinement step that would help the design teams show key aspects of their solutions to students, parents, and industry. In doing so the teams could solicit important feedback on what further details would be needed in their solutions to make them work. In a workshop, the design team members used the Story Spine Game (see figure 5.1) to develop the scripts for storyboards, which featured a key user of their community at the center of their solution.

"What If" Scenarios

It is possible to use storyboarding more informally, without creating visuals, by developing "what if" scenarios. Garth Nichols, vice principal for Student Engagement and Experiential Development at Havergal College, the independent all-girls K–12 school in Toronto, Canada, cleverly deployed "what if" scenarios into the conversation between students, teachers, and administrators. By using this verbal storyboarding technique, the group was able to decide which of their initial concepts could withstand further testing and which should probably be sent to the dustbin. Using "what if" scenarios in this way lets everyone on the team envision what their ideas could look like in reality without consuming a lot of time and resources. Here's what they did.

By the time the group of students, teachers, and administrators had completed their brainstorming phase they had landed on three major ideas for dealing with cellphone use in school. The immediate challenge now: Which of the three should they pilot?

Their "How Might We . . . ?" question was "How might Havergal College limit the use of personal devices to support wellness and community?" These were the three candidate solutions:

1. Block social media during class time.
2. Limit device access during the twenty-minute morning break from classes.
3. Ban personal devices in the dining hall or during common program time at the beginning or end of the day.

In their group meeting, they began to interrogate each of the solutions, going through the pros and cons of each, and spending a lot of time hammering out what each might look like, sound like, and feel like for students and faculty. By asking themselves, out loud, how each would work in practice, they sought to put themselves in the shoes of those who would experience them. They began to draw up scenarios.

They asked themselves, "What if we block social media during class time?" Then they invited staff from the information technology (IT) department to the meeting and asked them, "What would you have to do to make that happen?" The IT staff informed them that blocking social media was not feasible, notwithstanding the fact that students seem to be able to get around any type of network blocks.

They next asked themselves what it would look like if personal devices (smartphones and electronic tablets) were banned during the twenty-minute morning break, and this was deemed too short of a time to have any positive impact on wellness and community.

Some suggested an amalgamation of one or more of the ideas. One person proposed having a policy for grades 7 through 9 different from that for grades 10 through 12. They talked through what that would look like, sound like, and feel like. They realized it wouldn't feel good at all for students in grade 9, who would know they were being treated differently from students in grade 10. The emotions that scenario raised told the group their solution would need to be a universal approach.

One scenario suggested the solution involve banning personal devices at lunch break, and during before-school and after-school activities. As they talked that option through, the group concluded it would be going too far. So, they scaled that idea back a little bit. They decided on the following: Between the hours of 11:40 a.m. and 1:00 p.m., there would be no personal device use, regardless of where students were eating. This included the dining hall and classrooms that were used as spillover space during lunch. As Garth would later describe it, "Anytime we break bread."

This scaled-back version of the third prototype didn't feel as draconian as the original but still retained some of the redeeming features they sought:

- Encourage face-to-face communication during the lunch hour.
- Promote the life skill of having face-to-face conversations.
- Provide a break from screen time.
- Stimulate face-to-face social interaction with peers.

"What if" scenarios are a useful strategy that allows people around the table to envision what a solution could look like in a live setting.

EXPERIENTIAL PROTOTYPES

The second tool is an experiential prototype. In this prototype you carry out some aspect of the solution in a live setting where users can experience it firsthand. In a school where I advised on applying design thinking to the challenge of redesigning the school schedule, the teachers and students on the design team had several innovative ideas they prototyped through skits, paper grids, and storyboards. But none answered the question that was burning within the team: What would a new schedule look like in practice? What would the students do? How would they move about? And perhaps most important, how would they feel about it? The team decided to do a trial run of the prototype school schedule with a portion of the student body one day. The conditions under which users could see themselves in the solution and react to it could only be created by trying out the solution live. That's when you consider doing an experiential prototype. A team of teachers and three hundred students associated with those teachers elected to try out the new schedule on a Friday morning. I'll attempt to describe it here, but as I noted above, one of the reasons they decided to do an experiential prototype is because nonexperiential portrayals just aren't able to give observers, let alone users, the feel of actual experience. The schedule was essentially a matrix of twenty-two-minute time blocks, which when stacked together formed periods of time devoted to subject areas. Some subject areas were accorded one block of time; others received two or three. Students did not attend all the same classes. Those determinations were made based on hundreds of user interviews the design team conducted among students and teachers. A practical implication of the prototype design was that not all students would be changing classes at the same time since some classes lasted longer than others. On the day of the experiential prototype, in a high school of 1,800 students, the bell schedule was suspended so three hundred students could move through the morning trying out the new schedule while the other 1,500 students went about their day as usual. To the surprise of many, all students moved from class to class without the bells, and the design team, students, and teachers learned numerous things about the prototype schedule they could not have known otherwise. They learned that students can leave class and make it to the next class without bells. They discovered that bells actually contribute to congestion because students congregate in corridors until the last possible moment before the bell rings. Without any bells, students kept moving. Students from the journalism club roamed the halls that day to capture "person on the street" interviews with the users. They learned the students appreciated calmer hallways, more time in subjects that deserved it (e.g., language immersion courses and science classes), and a schedule that felt tailored to their learning interests. They also realized that the logistics of assigning teachers and students to such a flexible schedule would be challenging at full scale, so ultimately, the school adopted a modification of the prototype schedule that still allowed for an increase in student choice. And, perhaps most interestingly, the bells were never turned back on. Much later, when word spread in the community that a public urban high school had suspended bells to signal the start and stop of classes, school leaders from around the region sought out the school principal—they too wanted to know how they could drop bells from their school. The other school leaders must have thought there was a recipe to it. Well, there was, and what they were told was "Go interview two hundred students."

This schoolwide effort deserved the attention of a larger, experiential prototype. But one could imagine simpler experiential prototypes being deployed by grade-level teams or even by one teacher where a design team is interested in exploring how different classroom configurations might improve student engagement, or comfort, or collaboration. For instance, a volunteer teacher could offer to change the arrangement of the desks and furniture to test how well different patterns suit different goals.

Feedback on Experiential Prototypes

For experiential prototypes, design teams can use a feedback protocol like the one described below. Set up the prototype so several users can go through the motions of your experience, be it a class, new schedule, or other change. The general steps for gathering feedback are similar to those for a storyboard:

1. Explain what's going on.
2. Run the pilot experience.
3. Gather feedback.

Explain What's Going On

Say the following in your own words:

> Let me tell you a bit about the needs we discovered and what we're trying to address.
>
> • We want to *[describe the design challenge in one sentence]*.

- Our question is "How might we *[insert your 'How might we' question here]*?"
- We discovered the following unmet needs:
  – [List a few of the key unmet needs or insights that drove the prototype development.]
- For the next bit of time *[e.g., class period, hour, afternoon]*, I'd like to
  – Have you experience the *[classroom, schedule, space, etc.].*
  – Talk with you afterward to get your reactions.
  – Ask you to rank some other solutions we considered.

  Ready to begin?

After the user has toured or experienced the prototype, ask questions like this, always following up with "why?":

- What should we keep in here? What do you like?
- What should we increase? Should there be more of anything?
- What should we delete or get rid of?
- What, in this solution, meets *[describe the unmet need]* and what does not?
- What information have we missed in all this?
- Is this just for *[user category; e.g., parents]* or is it for *[a different user category; e.g., teachers]* as well?

"FAKE IT" PROTOTYPES

"Fake it" prototypes are the portrayal of complex or potentially expensive solutions in simple ways by "faking" them on paper or other media (e.g., presentation software). For instance, if a potential solution is a mobile phone app, you can "fake" the screens of the app and the interactivity within it on paper by creating a template of a blank mobile phone and drawing each screen in succession to portray what will happen. "Fake it" prototypes are especially good for testing several options as a solution. In a design challenge I worked on with colleagues at my university, for example, we sought to turn waits that caregivers typically experience with children (such as at bus stops) into learning time; we did this by providing subtle nudges via community signage to help parents leverage daily routines to increase their child's language skills. When we reached the prototyping stage, we wanted to learn if signage in the community could be used to prompt caregivers to have more conversations with their children during gap times. While metal signage posted in the community is expensive to manufacture, as are industrial decals that can be affixed to concrete sidewalks or asphalt pathways, we had many questions that needed answering before we spent one dime on signs. Would caregivers even look at our signs? If they did, would the wording catch their attention? How big would the signs have to be? And so on. We opted to create paper signage, which, while not durable over time, offered the flexibility of our being able to try different options quickly, to A/B test signs with users (compare two versions side by side), and even rule out settings where our solution would probably never work.

Feedback on "Fake It" Prototypes

For "fake it" prototypes, design teams can use a feedback protocol like the one described below. The general steps are:

1. Explain what's going on.
2. Show the "fake it" prototype.
3. Rank alternative solutions (have on hand a list of the options that were considered but not prototyped).

Explain What's Going On

Say the following in your own words:

> Let me tell you a bit about the needs we discovered and what we're trying to address.
> - We want to *[describe the design challenge in one sentence]*.
> - Our question is "How might we *[insert your 'How might we' question here]*?"
> - We discovered the following unmet needs:
>   - [List a few of the key unmet needs or insights that drove the prototype development.]
> - In our time together, I'd like to:
>   - Give you a tour of our prototype and get your reactions.
>   Ready to begin?

After the user has toured the prototype, ask questions like this, always following up with "why?":

- What should we keep in here? What do you like?
- What should we increase? Should there be more of anything?
- What should we get rid of?
- What, in this solution, meets *[describe the unmet need]* and what does not?
- What information have we missed in all this?
- Is this just for *[user category; e.g., parents]* or is it for *[a different user category; e.g., teachers]* as well?

When creating "fake it" prototypes, you don't limit yourself to paper. Dan Ryder's students at Mt. Blue High School used "fake it" prototypes and a 3D printer to create a set of handheld fidget toys designed to meet the needs of students with autism, attention deficit, and anxiety disorders. Dan's students interviewed fellow students in the school's day treatment program, which supports students with emotional and behavioral disorders, and in the school's special education program. They interviewed student caseworkers, school administrators, school counselors, nurses, and their own families.

The students worked in teams to design handheld toys they thought would work based on evidence they had developed in the need finding phase. They came up with eight toy styles, which were rapidly prototyped on a 3D printer. When the time came to field test the eight, the students went back out to their user base to conduct feedback interviews. They also placed some prototypes in the school counseling office and in the administrators' offices for two weeks. The staff in those offices agreed to keep track of how many times any of them were touched, handled, or played with. The students kept the data tracking simple: all the staff had to do was place a checkmark on a sheet whenever a student who happened to be in their offices touched one of the toys. This gave the student team a second layer of feedback data that was different from the direct opinions they collected in their prototype interviews. With the toys on display in a passive setting, they could gain insight on their aesthetic value as perceived by users. They refined their ideas based on the feedback they received and landed on three final designs that they took to market.[4] Which designs made the cut? One is called the Focus Clicker. It simulates the action of clicking a retractable pen without the clicking noise. Another, called the Focus Burger, is a thumb-sized device you can twist back and forth with two hands. Think of a slice of cheese sandwiched between two hamburger patties, all between two buns. Its multitextured design is a sensorial treat for the right person. And the third is the Focus Wheel, which is a simple hub held between the thumb and middle finger with a wheel you can spin with the index finger. As a matter of fact, its final design was an accident. The Focus Wheel was designed to be a large toy but was accidentally printed too small on the 3D printer. The team then realized that the small version was adorable and easier to use. Sometimes serendipity steps in to deal a friendly hand.

WHAT ABOUT IDEAS YOU DIDN'T PROTOTYPE?

Did you have several solutions from the brainstorm harvest that the group felt were promising? You may not have prototyped those, but you may want some insight on their viability in addition to the one solution you did prototype. Or perhaps you want to test several potential solutions at one time. Hand the user a list of the alternative solutions the team developed that were not prototyped. Then say, in your own words, "On this sheet is a list of alternative solutions we have thought of. Please mark, with a number, the top three solutions you think would be useful."

If, as they read the list, they say something like, "By X, do you mean Y?," you say, "What would you like it to be?" or "What would be ideal for you?" and then write down everything they say. Remember, you want to understand the solutions from the user's point of view.

After they rank the list, say, "Now I'd like to briefly hear why you selected the three alternatives that you did. Tell me why those were most important to you." Write down everything they say (see the sidebar).

Here are some insider tips to help with the feedback process.

- Be conversational. To that end, make sure you have prepared so it doesn't feel to the user that you are just reading off of a sheet of paper.

Alternative Solutions

Please rank the top three alternative solutions and add your own under "Other."

RANKING	ALTERNATIVE
	[Description of Alternative 1]
	[Description of Alternative 2]
	[Description of Alternative 3]
	[Description of Alternative 4]
	[Description of Alternative 5]

What's missing from this list that you'd love to see? Please list your ideas below.

	Other
	Other
	Other

- Ask "why?" all the time. You can vary the way you ask it with different versions of the same question—for example, "Why is that?," "What's behind that thought?," "How so?," or "Why do you feel that's the case?"
- Remember, you do not know everything about the direction of the prototype and what the next iteration will look like. Therefore, if users ask, as they engage with the prototype, something like "Will it do X or Y?," do not answer but rather reply with this question: "Would you like it to do X or Y?" Follow up with "why?" after their response.
- Use the information gleaned from the feedback round to determine what changes or improvements should be made to the prototype or if new prototypes should be created. Remember, the point is to learn. Do not spend money or time on additional prototypes until you have clarity on the key questions you need answered about your solution.

TWO TOOLS FOR FEEDBACK ON ANY PROTOTYPE: WARMS AND COOLS AND PLUS/DELTA

Kurtis Peterson, primary school principal at the International School of Ho Chi Minh City (ISHCMC), uses a friendly feedback technique called "warms and cools," which is an ideal way to obtain quick feedback on a prototype or event. Anyone can facilitate a warms and cools feedback session. The facilitator starts by saying something like, "Let's get some warms and cools about this idea we just reviewed." Then the facilitator gives each person in the room a chance to provide just one to five words of warm and cool feedback. Warm feedback can include comments about how well the idea addresses unmet needs, aligns with user goals, and so forth (things to turn up). Cool feedback might include desired elements that were missing from the solution, or perceived gaps in the ideas (things to turn down).

The plus/delta approach to formative feedback on prototypes, processes, and events is used by teachers across Fleming County Schools in Flemingsburg, Kentucky, where superintendent Brian Creasman works to make sure it remains ingrained in the culture. The plus/delta approach is an abbreviated version of the plus/delta/questions/ideas quadrant described in appendix B. Whereas the quadrant version has four areas for response, the plus/delta has only two. Like the warms and cools technique, anyone can facilitate a plus/delta. It can be done orally, by polling a group, or in writing, using sticky notes. Pluses are things that worked, or inspirational aspects of a prototype or process that can be built upon. Deltas are opportunities for improvement. When comments are captured on sticky notes, participants can post them on the wall where they can be clustered by theme and discussed openly by the group to better understand priorities for action.

CHALLENGES AND ADVICE IN THE PROTOTYPING PHASE

This phase tends to be very energizing to teams. It's a time when teams are generating a lot of ideas and becoming excited about moving from the realm of what's possible to what will become real. I heard one design team once refer to this stage as the point when pretend-like situations can become real. They invented a word for this: "pliking" (shorthand for "pretend-like"). They said they "pliked" a lot.

In this phase the team members develop creative solutions that are designed to make someone's life better.. This prospect tends to be exciting to team members because it's a moment when the effort of seeing the world from the user's viewpoint finally pays off. It's a point in the cycle when team members begin to see their work come full circle, and it brings into clear view why all the steps leading up to this point were necessary.

In the feedback stage, team members find it very rewarding to hear the positive reactions to the prototypes and helpful advice from the users.

Despite all these positives, some teams may find it hard to wrap their minds around creating an actual prototype of a solution. More often than not, prototypes don't take long to build (remember, they are supposed to be rough, rapid models). If it feels as though the team is trapped in a long buildup to make a prototype, just jump in and start making something. Because we prototype to learn and to think, making the leap to "the physical" helps teams really understand the challenges.

It's always advantageous to receive feedback from many different users because they can help catch issues with a prototype that might go undetected if you show the prototype to just one type of user. For instance, you may have a prototype that is aimed at making students' lives better, but the implementation and management of the solution may fall on the shoulders of certain teachers or administrators. Knowing their thoughts on the prototype will be important.

Let trial and error be your friend when prototyping. Refining a storyboard is a lot like refining any written story—determining the tone and which details to include takes lots of revision.

While in the feedback phase, don't forget to explain to users the backstory behind the prototype. This means you should let the user know about the unmet needs that were discovered in the design journey and how the prototype's features are designed to address those needs. In doing so, don't sell or advocate the solution—just indicate how the solution was derived. Leaving out the backstory may lead to less rich feedback.

Based on the feedback, parts of the team's proposal may have to be cut. This is yet another point in the process where it's useful to remember that the team's ideas should be thought of as "strong opinions weakly held." Not everything can make it into the final mix. It's also perfectly fine to have multiple prototypes and ask users which ones they think would be most useful.

If, after obtaining feedback from users about a prototype, the team has unanswered questions or is not sure what direction to take, test the prototype with more users and incorporate some of the remaining unanswered questions in the test sessions.

Test the most basic aspects of your solution first instead of offering a complex, multifaceted set of ideas. Then you can consider how adding new facets could enhance the solution.

WHAT'S NEXT?

In this phase you put one or more promising ideas out into the world as fast, low-fidelity prototypes. Thanks to the feedback you collected, you were able to improve on those ideas and turn them into something more viable. Next, you have the opportunity to pilot test an idea that you think could go to scale in the implementation phase.

CHAPTER **6**

IMPLEMENTATION

The goal for the teachers at Jackson Elementary was to enhance student agency through authentic student input. They surmised that if students had more opportunities for movement, their engagement in class would increase. At Jackson, core instruction tends to happen in the morning because the kids are more attentive at that time of day. However, the teachers knew that the students rarely leave the classrooms until lunchtime, which is 11:40 a.m. Once at lunch, they increase their movement, and after lunch they go to "specials" (e.g., art, PE, music, library). Then at 1:20 they go to recess. For a large part of their afternoon the students are busy moving, but they have no such activity in the morning.

The innovation team at Jackson Elementary met to create a theory of change statement and a logic model to help plan the implementation of morning movement. Principal Lori Mills explained to the team that because they were going to develop these, the team would be reaching consensus on what problem they were trying to solve and how they believed they would solve it. They would also have a plan that could easily be shared across the school before implementation to get input on potential improvements or advice on unforeseen barriers.

The theory of change statement the team developed went as follows:

Morning Movement. Enhancing student physical activity at Jackson Elementary. A design team, utilizing results from the need finding, synthesis, and prototyping stages of a design thinking cycle, discovered students may not have sufficient time in the morning for physical activity. The team discovered that students who are subjected to long periods of instruction tend to wane in their engagement with material, peers, and teachers. The team also heard how students wish to have more opportunities to physically move during the day but feel unable to do so due to the school's curriculum and schedule. If we can adjust the schedule and curriculum, students could have a period of time in the morning for physical movement. If students can have time for physical movement in the morning, they are more likely to be engaged with the material taught in late morning. Students who are more engaged with the material will be more successful in attaining academic outcomes.

After morning movement had been implemented for a while, Samantha, a fourth-grade teacher at Jackson Elementary, ran into Pete, a fifth-grade teacher.

"How's that pilot recess going? Are you noticing anything in class?" Pete asked.

"Yes, definitely," Samantha responded. "You know, before this we were covering so much content in the morning without a break. The kiddos just couldn't focus like I knew they could, especially in reading. I tried flexible grouping, small-group activities, everything. Whole group? Forget it. In the end what I concluded is we just had a hot-fudge sundae of learning going on for three hours in the morning. Now, with morning movement in place, I noticed how much more engaged the students are—they're interested in the readings, they're listening to one another. It's a new world."

A team from the state department of education did eventually visit Jackson Elementary to see the morning movement in action. The visit resulted in the school's being featured in the state teacher magazine. The fourth graders who were part of the need finding process the previous year were now fifth graders and were able to see the fruits of the process. Teachers followed up with students periodically to keep a conversation alive regarding how they felt about the recess break and what could be done to meet their needs further. They asked questions of the students like, "Is

*it working for you?" "Does it help you think more clearly when you're in
class?" "Do you look forward to your next movement break?"*

*The teachers also made sure the students knew that there was now
a second recess at Jackson Elementary because the kids said they needed
one. The piloting of the morning movement concept set the groundwork
for Principal Mills to take the idea to scale and have the morning recess
approved as part of the official school day.*

Design thinkers work iteratively, devising innovations to address challenges faced by their users. Some innovations deserve to be scaled up. Some don't. In this chapter we examine the process of taking a prototype and implementing it in a pilot project. By tracking the results of the pilot project, school leadership teams can decide if the project deserves to be a permanent part of a school's offerings.

In this chapter you will learn how to put together the implementation team and conduct a pilot test of a solution. What's different about this phase from the phases that precede it is the role of the design team. In the implementation phase there is a likelihood that the design team will not be the implementation team. Let's talk about why this may be the case (and why, in some instances, it should be the case).

IDENTIFY THE IMPLEMENTATION TEAM

Design teams draw their members from a pluralistic set of stakeholders, and may include participants from outside the school, such as parents or community members. The team may include insiders who play a role for their specialized knowledge on a topic—say, students, for their knowledge of their own school experience. The challenges design teams address often touch on matters related to policies and practices within the school, like the school schedule, the configuration of interior space, improving community partnerships, or reimagining the curriculum. Such challenges deserve the attention of pluralistic design teams because diversity of thought and experience, when applied in the context of a design cycle, yields solutions to challenges that are more creative, innovative, and useful to users. That said, implementation of those solutions generally should not be the purview of the design team. Why?

One reason is that at this stage the cycle has shifted from eliciting key voices for the purpose of developing promising solutions to a school challenge to implementation of that solution into the day-to-day work-ings of a complex organization. In other words, it has moved from a de-sign approach to more of an organizational management approach with an eye toward redesign as needed. From a practical standpoint, one can look at it this way: if the challenge being addressed involves redesigning a school's day pattern, there is a strong case to be made to have students and parents on that design team. There is not a strong case that the students and parents should be left to implement the new day pattern. Fine, you say, that's easy to understand. But suppose there are teachers on the design team. Shouldn't they, as school employees, implement the solution? In the case of solutions involving something as complex as the day pattern, no. Why would we expect teachers to lead a pilot project to implement a new school schedule when that is a feature of schools that is managed across several offices in the school and the district office? Thus, be thoughtful about who the most appropriate people are to implement a solution; they may not be those who have been designing it.

The implementation phase in a design cycle is well served by tenets of program design and program evaluation. Essentially, implementation is about selecting the most promising prototype and determining how to take it to scale, and then keep an eye on how it's going. You could think of it as a long-term live prototype but with fewer iterations. These longer-term prototypes are referred to as learning launches,[1] mini-pilots,[2] or simply pilots. For our purposes I'll refer to them as pilot programs. To think about implementation of your solution, I recommend tackling the implementation of your pilot program in three steps:

1. Ask yourselves some orienting questions.
2. Plan the rollout and evaluation of the pilot program.
3. Evaluate the pilot program.

ORIENT YOURSELF TO THE PILOT PROGRAM

The first step in this process is creating a short working document I call a face sheet. The face sheet is where you capture the key elements that need to be clear when developing a pilot program. The elements may not sound surprising to you; they are the classic five Ws: who, what, where, when, and why. The five Ws are often coupled with "how" at the end. We'll cover that in its own section because "how" requires a bit more room than a section of a face sheet.

To create a face sheet, there are two steps. Here's what you'll need to get started.

Materials and Time Needed to Complete a Face Sheet
- The face sheet worksheet (figure 6.1)
- The design team
- Possible implementers outside the design team who bring key skills
- Time needed for this step: 45 minutes

Face Sheet Components

Who: There are two "whos" on the face sheet: who benefits from the pilot program (who is the target user), and who will run the pilot program. Your pilot program is designed to make someone's life better, so keep that person, or group of people, at the center of your pilot. As for running the pilot, choose someone, or a pair of people, who can manage the tasks associated with launching, tracking, and communicating about the pilot. Remember, whatever is not tended to will wither. Read ahead to see what sorts of tasks are expected of people who are assigned to run a pilot program.

What: Nailing down the "what" involves giving the pilot program a name and providing a short description of what the pilot program is designed to do. Two sentences can cover it. Start with one sentence on what will happen in the solution (what you will do). If you feel the solution played out in the pilot program requires more than one sentence to describe, resist the urge to list every detail you'll do—keep it succinct. You'll have plenty of space to plan out all the details in the "how" section of the pilot program planning. End with a sentence on the expected outcomes that will occur as a result of running the program.

Where: Describe in one sentence the setting where the pilot program will take place.

Figure 6.1 Face sheet worksheet

WORKSHEET   IMPLEMENTATION PHASE

Face Sheet

Pilot program title

Who benefits from the pilot program (who is the primary user)?

Who will run the pilot program?

What is the pilot program designed to do?

Where will the pilot program take place? What is the setting?

When will the pilot run? When does it start? Stop?

Why this now?

When: Write down the start and stop dates of the pilot.

Why: Describe why this solution was selected for a pilot program. You can refer to the overarching needs and insights the team discovered in the design process, in what ways the features of this solution meet those needs, and any other features of the solution that made it an optimal choice for elevating it to pilot status.

PLAN THE PILOT

The second step in the process is planning the rollout and evaluation of the pilot program. Let's say, for example, you are part of a design team situated in a middle school. After going through the need finding and synthesis phases, the team arrives at new insights about the nature of the relationships students in the school have with adults, particularly teachers and staff. The team discovers students may be resisting forming relationships with adults in the school. The team finds that teachers are spread too thin to allow for time to foster quality relationships with students. The team also hears from the students that they actually yearn to have quality relationships with the adults in the school but feel thwarted by the day pattern, peer pressure, and an overall feeling of not enough time to get any one thing done well.

Let's suppose that an idea that was prototyped in the last phase is an advisory program. Advisory programs are set periods of time within a school day where teachers and staff can work with students on issues not generally covered in the academic day.[3] Let's say in our example this idea made it to the pilot program stage after the solution was depicted in a storyboard and shown to students and staff. Based on the feedback gained on the storyboard, a teacher volunteered to prototype an advisory program live in her classroom for one week. She rearranged how each of her class periods unfolded to allow time for a mini advisory program in her classes. Along the way she asked her students how they felt about the advisory portion of class, focusing on whether the unmet needs identified in need finding, synthesis, and even in early prototyping were being addressed. In the process a great deal was learned about what could and couldn't be done in an advisory program in addition to an overwhelming sense that the outcomes were very positive. The team took this information to the school leadership and worked on a pilot program design. After completing a face sheet for the pilot project, they developed a detailed "how" document by using a tool called a theory of change.

CREATE A THEORY OF CHANGE

A theory of change is simply a theory of how and why your pilot program will work.[4] It's the sequence of events expected to create the change that will help meet the needs discovered in the design process. A good theory of change is depicted in two ways: in narrative form and graphically, in what's called a logic model. Let's see how both of these play out in the example above for a pilot advisory program.

Narrative Version of a Theory of Change

A narrative version of a theory of change unfolds as a series of if-then statements based on the overarching need discovered by the design team. By writing out a theory of change statement in such a fashion, one is able to determine if the pilot program has "face validity" (makes sense on its face). It also has the advantage of being easy to share with students and colleagues, allowing them to provide feedback on where gaps may exist or where details need to be added. Here's an example:

> An advisory program for middle school students. A design team, utilizing findings from the need finding, synthesis, and prototyping stages of a design thinking cycle, discovered that students may be resisting forming relationships with adults in the school. The team found that teachers are spread too thin to allow for time to foster quality relationships with students. The team also heard how students yearn to have quality relationships with adults in the school but feel thwarted by the day pattern, peer pressure, and an overall feeling of not enough time to get any one thing done well. If we have the time and resources to meet with students in an advisory capacity, then teachers and staff can work with students on issues that are not generally covered in the academic day. If teachers and staff can work with students on issues not covered in the academic day, then they can make better personal connections with students. By making better personal connections with the students, they can address issues that may be barriers to im-

portant outcomes such as attendance, school liking, social choices, and academic performance.

Here is the example, again, with annotations before each component to show the structure:

[Short descriptive title] An advisory program for middle school students. *[A statement of who did what and what the chief discovery was]* A design team, utilizing findings from the need finding, synthesis, and prototyping stages of a design thinking cycle, discovered that students may be resisting forming relationships with adults in the school. *[Statements on potential causes for what was discovered]* The team found that teachers are spread too thin to allow for time to foster quality relationships with students. The team also heard how students yearn to have quality relationships with adults in the school but feel thwarted by the day pattern, peer pressure, and an overall feeling of not enough time to get any one thing done well. *[A statement describing the opportunity]* If we have the time and resources to meet with students in an advisory capacity, teachers and staff can work *[Output]* with students on issues that are not generally covered in the academic day. *[Intermediate outcome]* If teachers and staff can work with students on issues not covered in the academic day, then they can make better personal connections with students. *[Long-term outcome]* By making better personal connections with the students, they can address issues that may be barriers to important outcomes such as attendance, school liking, social choices, and academic performance.

Create a Logic Model

Couple this narrative with a graphic depiction of your theory of change, called a logic model (see figure 6.2). A logic model is a graphic depiction of your theory of change showing explicit linkages that you believe exist in your pilot program, from resources to outputs to outcomes.[5]

Figure 6.2 Logic model template

By depicting a theory of action in such a way, one is able to see the component parts of the pilot program as objects that can be measured for their success. Let's look at an instance of a logic model using the example of the advisory program (see figure 6.3).

In general, there are two levels of success one should be interested in when planning and evaluating a pilot program: implementation success and outcome success.

Implementation Success

Implementation success pertains to the level to which one carries out the steps that are expected to lead to the outcomes. If implementation, as measured by inputs, is not faithful to the promising aspects of the prototype, or the level of implementation is insufficient, then it cannot be expected that the outcomes will be reached. For instance, in the example above regarding the advisory program, if an insufficient number of advisory meetings are held, or none are scheduled at all, then it cannot be said that the pilot program was successfully implemented. A fair and faithful effort to implement the program as designed is required so the pilot team can decide if the desired outcomes were brought about.

Figure 6.3 Logic model for the advisory program

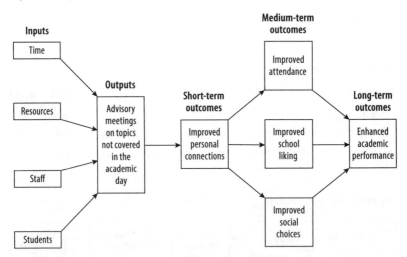

Outcome Success

Outcome success pertains to the level at which expected outcomes are attained. Outcomes are the changes in behavior sought as a result of meeting the needs of the users. For our example of the advisory program, the outcomes can be found in the last sentence of the theory of change narrative: *attendance, school liking, social choices, and academic performance.*

A Logic Model Helps Verify Face Validity, Set Indicators, and Track Success

Logic models should not be considered static depictions of a pilot program; rather, they are living documents that should be adjusted on the fly. Think of them as visual prototypes of your pilot program. If any part of the logic model seems too simplistic, revise the model so it includes the specificity needed. If it doesn't make sense that a certain outcome would flow from a particular output, reconsider what should logically occur. Just like any prototype, no program pilot survives its first contact with a user, so be prepared to adjust the plans you have made once you kick off the pilot.

Logic models help team members set indicators for success to determine what parts of the program are working well and whether outcomes have been reached. If we were to refer to the boxes in a logic model as the "elements," I recommend selecting one or more indicators of success for each element (box) in the logic model. Common examples of indicators include the presence or existence of something (or not); rate or frequency of participation; attitudes toward or perceptions of an element; and the increase, decrease, existence, or absence of certain behaviors. For instance, in the advisory program example, an indicator of success for the "resources" element (in the input column) might be whether the materials the teachers and staff needed to hold an advisory meeting were created and were of sufficient quality. An indicator for success for the element entitled "improved school liking," in the short-term outcomes column, might be favorable responses by students on a survey of school satisfaction after participation in the advisory program for a set number of sessions.

When tracking indicators of success for the pilot program, make sure you are collecting data that tells you not only if the pilot is supporting the unmet needs of users, but also collecting data on how well the program can be implemented in the system and culture of the school. Consider adjustments to either the pilot program or the broader school structure that would enable the program to be successful (particularly aspects you are certain are contributing to meeting the user needs).

REINVOLVE THE DESIGN TEAM

After a predetermined amount of time, reconvene the design team and users to revisit the implementation, and discuss whether the user experienced the solution as you predicted in the narrative theory of change, and whether the capabilities you had (or your partners had) were sufficient to carry out the solution successfully. If yes, but the solution was lackluster, talk about why that might be the case. Discuss whether the key questions you hoped would be answered were indeed answered. Bring in relevant stakeholders to consider how to transfer the ownership of the solution from the design team to a more stable and formal portion of the organization. Make any necessary corrections to the solution and implement an iteration.

Here are some signs that it's time to bring the team back together (all of which are good signs that you're paying attention to feedback):

- Team members become disengaged.
- You can't tell if the pilot is working or not.
- You don't feel like you're getting the results you deserve given your investment of time and resources.
- The target users aren't using the solution.

When you decide to reconvene the team, here are some questions to discuss. Remember, your ideas are not precious, and your implementations do not have to be perfect. It's the feedback you garner, and how you iterate upon it, that's the gold.

- Did we get the result we anticipated?
- Did we implement the pilot with the right people?

- Did we implement with fidelity—did we do what we said we would do?

The Pilot at Fairdale

The educators at Fairdale Elementary prototyped a way to keep the best parts of being a compassionate school and include PE in the curriculum. Bringing PE back into the schedule meant giving up the one of the school's compassion classes. But what worked in their favor was the fact that the PE teacher, who was an innovative, well-regarded educator, had been the teacher previously assigned to teach the compassion class. PE was put back on the schedule and the PE teacher was keen to integrate the compassion philosophies from the old course into the new PE curriculum. And, in a bit of serendipity, an opportunity opened up for Fairdale to return to its foreign language magnet status. The additional class section that opened up after Fairdale opted away from the formal compassion classes allowed the school to bring Spanish back into the curriculum.

The educators at Fairdale feel as though they have been able to meet two key needs expressed by the students: continue cultivating a compassionate school community and provide us with opportunities to be well through physical activity and foreign language.

After PE was returned to the curriculum at Fairdale Elementary, Erin Coyle sought feedback from the students on how they felt about the change. She put the following question to the students: "Think about some of the things that have been done differently this year at Fairdale. How do you feel about these changes?" This open-ended question did not steer the students to any particular change at the school, and yet, in the 144 responses, students overwhelmingly remarked how the presence of PE made them happy. They were also happy to have a Spanish teacher.

This told Erin and the teachers at Fairdale they were on the right track, that the big blocks that represented the change, bringing back PE and a foreign language, were still the right ones. This allowed Erin and the team to focus on iterative improvements within that framework and to focus on integrating the instructional approaches the Fairdale instructional community wanted to see, such as a workshop model across grades and subjects.

It also told Erin that the students felt as though they were really heard.

The Pilot at Havergal

Havergal College, an independent K–12 girls school in Toronto, Canada, has implemented a schoolwide pilot of the new personal device policy: between the hours of 11:40 a.m. and 1:00 p.m., there will be no use of personal devices wherever students eat. The school has sought feedback from parents, teachers, and students. A recent schoolwide survey contained the question, "How well is the new personal device policy working?" It garnered a 3.7 on a scale of 1 to 5, with 1 meaning not going well and 5 meaning going well.

Many parents told the school they appreciated the new policy for its intent to foster an increase in face-to-face interaction. Some parents did point out, however, that the lunch break was the time when they need to reach their daughter on her personal phone to confirm afterschool pickup or dropoff for sports or other activities.

Faculty have started to become cognizant of the new opportunities the policy affords them in terms of interacting with students and have come up with new ways to redirect a student who is in breach of the policy. For instance, Garth Nichols, the assistant principal, carries with him a mini game pad. When he finds a student on her phone, he sits down next to her and says, "Well, you just won yourself a game of Hangman with Mr. Nichols." Or he will sit with the student and start a conversation. One key metric, more qualitative than quantitative, is the increased noise in the dining hall. Here the impact of the policy is unmistakable. The din of conversation is higher than it's ever been while the students are in the hall.

One unintended artifact of the policy is that even though the lunch period lasts until 1:00 p.m., by 12:40 the dining hall is empty and the Havergal students are outside the designated eating zones and back on their phones. Garth keeps this in perspective. He knows that if students choose to eat their lunch quickly so as to be able to use their device before 1:00 p.m., that remains their decision. He also knows that the school, in an interest to guide their students in a healthy direction, articulated the new policy responsibly and intentionally with empathy toward those affected by the issue.

Havergal will continue to monitor how the policy looks and feels to its stakeholders and will continue to adjust as needed. At the end of the first year of implementation, Garth will convene a body of students from across the school to engage in an empathetic round of conversations, basically repeating the process he facilitated at the start of this initiative, to revisit whether they have been addressing the right challenge and determine if there are other solutions the school should consider to refine its policy.

Amount of Time for a Pilot

How much time should be devoted to implementing a pilot and studying the result? This can depend. At Fairdale Elementary and at Havergal College, they are taking the better part of a school year to watch how the implementation goes. Their solutions are predicated on seeing outcomes over time, some more effective than others. For instance, at Fairdale, their solutions involved installing new courses into the curriculum. It's generally not feasible to judge how well a new class is going in less time than a semester. Further, there are probably institutional metrics associated with judging course quality (e.g., teacher evaluations and other instructional supervision metrics) that are not generally applied until after the fact. In Havergal's case, there are affective outcomes they will seek to determine (e.g., how much people like the new personal device policy) that are best measured over time. Initial feelings toward a new policy that restricts personal device use by youth are likely to be different at the very start of implementation versus months out. On the other hand, there are suitable early metrics they can measure that can suggest success or failure of the policy, such as having faculty observe how many students are on their phone during the restricted period. In sum, take into account the urgency that is felt around having to "get it right." Meaning, ask yourself how soon you must know whether the solution you've put in place is working well or not.

CHALLENGES AND ADVICE IN THE IMPLEMENTATION PHASE

Pilot programs are valuable because they provide you with an opportunity to track the success of the solutions you have designed. Here is some advice on common challenges.

Strive to have pilot participants who match your target users. This ensures the feedback you collect will be more relevant.[6]

Pilot programs are live representations of dynamic solutions, and you can presume there will always be features of your pilot that will never survive first contact with a user. Assume there will be changes in the pilot (because there always are).

Pilot programs often provide the design and implementation team with ideas or approaches that were not foreseen before the pilot.[7] Assigning a team member to keep a journal of learnings from the pilot will ensure you don't forget important lessons from the pilot.

Keep in mind that the logic model doesn't tell you whether you are doing the right thing or whether you should even conduct the pilot you are conducting.[8] Your logic model represents how you believe the pilot will work if everything goes to plan.

Depending on the goal of the pilot program and the setting in which you implement it, challenges can arise if there are unique cultural or social norms surrounding the expectations on how the pilot should be carried out. For instance, if the pilot program is designed to support outcomes for school families who are culturally and linguistically diverse, you benefit from paying attention to issues that could influence expectations about the program and its likelihood of success. Examples of such issues include:

- Deeply rooted traditions and cultures around education
- Lack of trust of outsiders or "experts"
- Social beliefs around certain behaviors

Involving members from the target group on the pilot team helps enhance cultural competency, encourage participation, and reduce social stigmas. Materials for the pilot, including information packets, instructions, and feedback forms should all be culturally appropriate.[9]

WHAT'S NEXT?

In this chapter we discussed developing an implementation team for a pilot project. The team articulates the overarching aim of the pilot using a face sheet and plans the pilot articulating a theory of change. Creating a logic model from the theory of change helps the team identify the outcomes and guides what's important to measure. In the next and final chapter, I discuss broader issues of leadership, and how the practice of design thinking changes the ways educators think about problems.

CHAPTER 7

LEADERS AS DESIGNERS

I've seen school districts where approaches to problems were essentially adopted due to their success in another district. Perhaps you've seen this happen. A plan is proposed from near the top of the hierarchy and materials are acquired, but somewhere along the line the motivation needed from teachers and students doesn't materialize. When ideas are taken from other districts, they are not, by their nature, well suited to address the unmet needs in another district.

I've met high school students who feel it would be almost impossible to sit down with their principal and talk with them about school. They consider school leaders to be almost untouchable, out of reach, and disconnected to the students.

I've talked with teachers who work in districts where money is thrown at a cause, such as literacy, and multitudes of literacy materials are purchased to be shipped out to schools. And they tell me that it's in those schools where the materials end up sitting in closets, gathering dust. Who decided to purchase these materials? The teachers aren't sure. Did the district consult any of its school's leaders or teachers about what resources or support may have been needed to promote literacy? No. Did anyone check to see if those materials already existed at the school? No

one did. Did anyone ask educators at the schools if the materials supported the goal of literacy? Nope. Setting aside for the moment the sheer
financial cost, what does this say about the culture of a district and how
it is able to address the unmet needs of its community members?

In this chapter we will explore what I've seen when educators, particularly aspiring and current school leaders, are exposed to design
thinking. I'll introduce a framework that has been helpful to educators
as they establish how design thinking can play a role in creating change
in their schools, and I'll discuss how one can attain the mind-set of a
design thinker. I'll also answer some common questions I've entertained
over the years. I'll close with a few cases that illustrate the scope to which
design thinking can be applied in schools.

WHEN EDUCATORS ARE EXPOSED TO DESIGN THINKING

I've met many educators who, based on what they have heard or read
about design thinking, say, "Sounds good," showing chiefly benign interest. But I know that their inner monologue is simultaneously thinking,
"I don't want to learn something new among the myriad of approaches
thrown at me on a daily basis as a school leader."

That is, until they actually spend a few hours doing it.

My experience has been that when an educator engages in a design
process that includes empathizing with a user and designing something
that makes that user's life better, their embrace of design thinking as a
mind-set intensifies dramatically and their ability to find time to do it
miraculously increases.

How do I know this? For about a decade I've been teaching design
thinking at universities through either a semester-long course or as units
within my leadership classes. I've also been providing professional development to current and aspiring school leaders through the United States
and internationally. Through these experiences, adult educators design
for each other or design for students. And it's this exposure that counts.
It changes their outlook on how education can and should be designed
and delivered. Absent participating in such activities, my students and
workshop participants, who are educators, aspiring school leaders, and
sitting leaders, do not believe design thinking would have resonated with

them as much as it did had they only read about it. The design thinking workshops I've conducted, where adults work as equals with middle and high school students to solve a school-related problem, have been so impactful that educators go out the following week to start employing the strategy with their own preK–12 students. And some, despite having relatively lengthy careers in education, say that until they practiced design thinking with youth in my classes and workshops, they never imagined having their students take part in any decision-making process. (Some even remark they now feel a little foolish about that.)

Educators who learn design thinking find it eye opening to design for another person. My graduate students and workshop participants begin to realize just how often they do not ask students what they view as strengths and weaknesses of their school, nor do they ask what students need to succeed in that school. Educators who are design thinkers realize their students are in the trenches, seeing things no teacher or administrator can see.

By learning design thinking, students in my university classes find out where critical needs and failures in the system reside. In cases where my students have empathized with preK–12 students, the experience with design thinking made them realize that administrators are great at making plans, but are generally not well suited to searching out solutions.

As school leaders, educators discover that they need to find time to connect with students so they can obtain feedback on initiatives and truly understand the root of the problem in their schools. This is what makes design thinking such a powerful tool in understanding the issues within the education system for both teachers and students. At times, decisions are made based on the perceptions of people at the top who have not taken time to see what is happening at the bottom.

Educators realize that design thinkers try to get on the same level as those who actually experience the problems they are trying to solve. They seek input from the people who are most affected by the challenges that exist in the school. They don't look at themselves as the experts; rather, they look at the people they are trying to help as the experts.

When I have aspiring leaders act as designers by going through a design thinking cycle, they become privy to expertise held only by their students—priceless feedback the educators would not be able to know without asking, empathetically, about students' perspective.

By engaging in an authentic design thinking cycle, educators figure out that the issue is not always a lack of resources. Certainly, schools and communities deserve to be resourced; my point here is more about shining a light on new solutions to long-standing problems that don't start by throwing more money at them. Design thinking provides educators with a process by which they can look inside their own community as a resource for ideas, experience, and creativity. A wealth of knowledge and experience resides within every school and every district but lies relatively untapped because educators tend to spend more time planning for change than actually searching for ways to make it happen.

DESIGN THINKERS ARE SEARCHERS, NOT PLANNERS

Economist William Easterly suggests people can be either planners or searchers.[1] Let's look at the characteristics of planners versus searchers (see table 7.1).

What might this look like in schools? Let's take an example of a real challenge facing a school district: the implementation of a new computer application called Journey. A district has invested a lot of money in the

Table 7.1 Planners versus searchers

PLANNERS . . .	SEARCHERS . . .
Announce good intentions but don't motivate anyone to carry them out.	Find things that work and get some reward.
Raise expectations but take no responsibility for meeting them.	Accept responsibility for their actions.
Determine what to supply.	Find out what's in demand.
Apply global blueprints.	Adapt to local conditions.
Believe outsiders know enough to impose solutions.	Believe only insiders have enough knowledge to find workable solutions.
Search for utopian solutions and focus efforts on infeasible tasks.	Work to understand the unmet needs of those around them and craft solutions to meet those needs.

program and, after some encouraging experimentation, all teachers, preK–12, will be required to integrate the program into their curriculum this next school year.

There's one hitch. While there are teachers and students who are willing to use the program, there are also teachers and students who do not want to use it. Generally speaking, elementary teachers are on board with the program, but those in grades 7 through 12 are dragging their feet.

The planners in the district have sung the praises of the Journey program but haven't done anything to motivate teachers or students to implement it. They have high expectations for its use, but will take no responsibility if teachers and students don't meet them. The planners are relying on the program gurus—the vendors who sold the district the program—to impose solutions to the usage problem.

What would searchers do? Searchers would be in the trenches with the teachers and students to determine what was needed in the first place and either devise or select the best solution—whether it was Journey or not. Searchers would have listened to feedback from teachers and students. They would have held themselves accountable, even while admitting they didn't know the answers, but sought them using trial and error. Searchers also believe that only insiders have enough knowledge to find solutions, so, even if they decide Journey is the solution, they would not rely heavily on the software representatives but instead would listen to the teachers and students for guidance on what steps need the most attention during implementation.

Stories like these are not uncommon across schools. Substitute any solution you please for the Journey program above. Take the example of a school in the process of becoming a one-to-one laptop campus (one laptop per student). No teacher is clear on what is expected of them or how often the computers are supposed to be used in the classroom. The school is managed by planners who came up with the idea that the school's students each need a computer. They found the financing but neglected any guidelines for use.

Teachers in the school are talking with educators at other one-to-one laptop schools trying to figure out ways to make this transition as smooth as possible. As they do so, the planners watch from the sidelines, wondering why everyone is so uncomfortable with the change.

Fall arrived and so did the computers, only days before school began. The new school year started out with zero professional development for the staff and minimal instruction for the students. The planners believed that if you handed a teacher and a student a computer, they would automatically know how to use the various programs and utilize it as a learning tool. The planners also believed that students would be better prepared, and problems such as failing grades, absenteeism, and classroom management would improve substantially. The planners did not foresee how much this initiative needed more frontloading for its intended users. Planners believe in handing out a solution with hopes that someone will make it work, while a searcher believes it must be "homegrown" and developed by those it affects the most.

Most educators are planners. They have great ideas and big plans for improving student achievement. Easterly describes planners as those who "keep pouring resources into a fixed objective, despite many previous failures at reaching that objective, despite a track record that suggests the objective is infeasible or the plan unworkable." Design thinkers, however, have a searcher mentality, which Easterly describes as "agents for change in the alternative approach."[2]

I heard from one of my university students about a disconnect between the administration and the staff at her school. The teachers often feel in the dark as to why decisions get made. For example, an incentive program was put in place in which students with no missing assignments at the end of the second quarter would be able to view a movie during fifth and sixth periods. When the third quarter arrived, the administration changed the reward—movie viewings would be for any students receiving all As, Bs, or Cs. This incentive program was initiated without any input from teachers, who raised many concerns about the program. However, very few of those concerns were taken into consideration by the administration. This is a case of an administration having great intentions to inspire students to strive for a goal, but doing little to change students' motivation to work.

ARE YOU A PLANNER?

When exposed to design thinking, preK–12 educators start to reframe the way they see students and their own philosophy of teaching and learning. After going through the process of empathizing with some secondary students in my graduate class, one of my students noted that the experience had a tremendous impact on her educational philosophy. What my graduate student learned from being a designer, and then from reading about planners and searchers, was that while she may have had good intentions as she planned and taught in the classroom, she had always been more of a planner, and not a searcher. Until she practiced design thinking, my student had followed a philosophy of making sure every concept she taught was relevant to her students' lives. But she had done so through her own lens, not a student's lens. She had been a planner.

As an educator, have you ever chosen lessons or content and then related what you believed to be relevant to the students? Have you actually sat down with your students before planning your lessons to ask them what is relevant to them? Educators who get to practice design thinking no longer continue to plan instruction without speaking to their students. The students become part of the lesson-making process when teachers and administrators ask questions like these: Do you think what you are learning is valuable? Do you enjoy your class(es)? Do you feel like your teacher believes you are a valued member of your learning community? Do you feel a part of the decisions, that your feedback is solicited and then used to make changes?

HOW DO YOU ATTAIN A DESIGN THINKING MIND-SET?

I'm often asked, "How do you get the design thinking mind-set?" and, just as often, "How do you find the time?" On their face, these questions seem different—one, the mind-set question, is about learning and the other, finding the time, is more resource-related. But over the past ten years I've learned that the answer to both is that the time appears when you have the mind-set. Because once teachers, aspiring leaders, and sitting leaders get the right mind-set, they are so taken with design thinking's promise that they find the time to practice it. Finding time, after all, is not like mining minerals—you don't go off somewhere to find more of it. Finding time is about adjusting priorities and making choices. Its' a matter of settling in one's head what the payoffs are from engaging in any given activity. And what educators find is that once they've seen the promise of design thinking in action, their ability to "find time" to apply it increases because the perceived payoffs are so large.

DOES DESIGN THINKING WORK FOR BOTH SIMPLE AND COMPLEX CHALLENGES?

All schools face challenges. Some are well bounded; others are more open and complex. Whether the issue you face is tightly bounded, loosely coupled, simple, or complex, what really determines whether design thinking is suited for solving it is whether the challenge will let you leverage codesign with the people most affected by the problem, or with those who are traditionally left aside in the conversations about a solution. What's key to remember is that this is not an add-on to what you're doing, but a *process* by which you can do things. Design thinking is content-agnostic. It doesn't really care what you are working on. However, it does care that what you're working on is improved. Let's look at some samples.

Classroom-Based Challenges

If you are a teacher you may wonder, Can this process be applied at the classroom level? The answer is yes. A fair follow-up question is, Should design thinking be applied at the classroom level? As a teacher, you may view this as taking up a lot of time in the classroom, detracting from time spent on lessons, content, and standards. I think the easiest way to use design thinking in the classroom is to first ask your students what they think and feel about the lesson or content being presented, your teaching strategies, how the room is structured, or the different processes that occur in your classroom. Students can give input of what works for them and what they want or expect. Enter your classroom with a curious mind, asking yourself, What can I do for you to decrease your stress? How can I help you? What are you looking for?

When educators ask those kinds of questions, they start to see new ways of involving students. For instance, a teacher might be inspired by

the needs of her students to design a new playground. Or design a better backpack, create a shelving/storage system for a technologically advanced classroom, and so on. My graduate students see ways to practice
what author Jonathan Kozol calls mischievous irreverence to circumvent
the status quo.[3] Teachers who have learned to become design thinkers
are able to understand the lives and needs of their students, like Samantha, who in chapter 6 figured out how to test ways to get her students to
move more—within the guidelines of state regulations. She, like others,
used the expressed needs and interests of students to derive new solutions to sticky problems.

Parent Night

When educators are exposed to design thinking they come up with meaningful and beneficial new ways to apply its mind-sets without having to
engage in an entire design cycle. For instance, why not launch an activity
at a school family night built on the premise of design thinking? One
could conduct a session wherein teachers ask parents what they want their
child's education to look like and what goals they have for the school. A
design team could take all the information gained from such a session
and incorporate it into a staff development activity for teachers on how
parents view school, then stoke a discussion on where teacher, student,
and parent views about the goals of school are similar and different.

At the European League of Middle Level Educators (ELMLE) workshop, the challenge was, How might we improve middle-level parent-
teacher conferences at the American Overseas School of Rome? Nine
design teams focused on the needs of a composite peer teacher in the
workshop, empathetically understanding the challenges and unmet
needs from her point of view. In about an hour, the teams delivered
nine poster-sized sketches of unique prototype solutions for improving
parent-teacher conferences.

School Cleanliness

Recently, when my graduate students met with K–12 students to practice
design thinking, they learned how seemingly small things can be very
big deals to students. For instance, one of my graduate students asked a

high school student what the biggest problem was at her school. He was anticipating a response having to do with the classes offered, or a lack of connection between schooling and real life. But no. She was worried about the cleanliness of her school. She wanted clean silverware in the cafeteria, hairballs to be swept from locker room floors, and so on. While we don't want to overlook the big problems, there are many smaller challenges that won't be discovered unless we ask the students.

Student Voice

Some of the most powerful challenges I've encountered deal with the challenge of surfacing student voice. Brad Fiege, a social studies teacher in Greece Central Schools in New York, recalls how it struck him one day: attempts at improvement in his school didn't necessarily start with students. Rather, attempts at improvement usually began from a problem-solving stance on the part of the teachers. The model was much the same everywhere. Brad explained, "We form action teams and the teachers think about what is needed to solve the problem and we don't consult the end user." Then Brad and a colleague, Keena Smith, went to Los Angeles for a workshop on how to foster a school environment to support college and career readiness. What was different this time was the workshop facilitators' promotion of a design thinking approach to change. Brad said, "What we took away from that experience was how to reframe . . . problem solving [as a matter that] brought in the end user—that empathized with students. This was huge for me because it changed motivation into action."

Brad and Keena came back from the workshop and helped train their colleagues. They sought not to create discrete improvements here and there but to shift the culture of the building to one that values listening to each other. Over a span of three days, Brad, Keena, and their colleagues gathered with their district peers to reimagine student agency; they asked, How might we build student voice? Sixty-five educators formed ten design teams and in a large gathering they interviewed students, rapidly prototyped solutions to the student voice challenge, and tested the ideas in classrooms over the next three days. Three iteration rounds were held to refine the ideas. In the end, the district was able to do two important things: teach the design cycle and, along the way, demonstrate a way to integrate student voice into the school change process.

But what may be the most important outcome was a palpable shift in the mind-sets. Applying a design thinking cycle showed the group something important. "We discovered we truly do have the resources to solve great problems," Keena recalls. "That's huge!"

Titan Intern Day, a Student-Inspired Science Curriculum

The idea of a surgery day, known as Titan Intern Day in Greece Central School District, came into being after two teachers, a librarian and a science teacher, attended a design thinking training session.[4] There, they were exposed to the idea of uncovering students' desire to design meaningful learning experiences. After empathetically interviewing students, the staff learned students wanted more hands-on learning, and Titan Intern Day was born. Titan Intern Day is the culminating event marking weeks of work in which a group of Advanced Placement biology students lead their own learning by designing a surgery project for themselves each year. The students choose and research a medical problem that requires surgery, contact local surgeons for guidance, then design and build their own practice body and organs out of papier-mâché and clay and foam. Today they even use a 3D printer to make vertebrae, tumors, and other anatomical objects. Students must do their own networking to find the professionals who will teach them how to solve the medical problem. This has resulted, for some, in being invited to shadow medical professionals at work and view surgeries. On Titan Intern Day, the students receive scrubs and are loaned relevant equipment from a local teaching hospital; on surgery day, they set up about a dozen operating room stations. Younger biology students at each station serve as interns and take notes as older students describe the procedure being performed and any underlying biology concepts the student studied in preparation for the simulated operation. This large demonstration day of learning is attended by other teachers and administrators, parents, and community members.

MOSAICS, an Award Winning, Student-Designed, for-Credit Course and Diversity Club

MOSAICS, created by students for students, is a for-credit high school English course and diversity club in Greece Central School District. The path by which this course became a reality was paved with teacher empathy for student needs and, in turn, student discovery of the unmet needs of their peers. A high school teacher in the district who had been trained as a design thinker saw an opportunity while working with students who were designing a reading list of African American authors to celebrate Black History Month. The students lamented that the school lacked a course on African American history and culture. The teacher asked the students what they would want such a course to look like. Their answers turned into a broader need finding research, enlisting their peers to help envision what a course that encompassed diversity broadly might look like. The students worked to understand the needs of their peers in terms of what kind of curriculum would be relevant and responsive to the student community. Their empathetic need finding led to the creation of a prototype curriculum that included field trips, guest speakers, and collaboration with colleges. The prototype curriculum soon became an approved, for-credit course for seniors in the high school. Not wanting other grade levels to be turned away from the opportunity to access the curriculum, MOSAICS also became a sanctioned school club for all students. Soon, two more sections opened up and a MOSAICS club was founded for those in the district who do not have the course in their school. The club provides a forum for high school students to meet regularly to examine issues of race, religion, gender, and poverty. In 2016 the MOSAICS program received the Princeton Prize for creating a forum for diversity that is part of the curriculum as well as a club to critically examine and celebrate inclusion.

District Transformation

Eminence Independent School District was not always, well, eminent, at least not from an education standpoint. When Buddy Berry became superintendent, Eminence, Kentucky, had a population of 2,498. The single-building district had an enrollment of 638 students.[5] Of those, 70 percent were eligible for a free or reduced-price lunch. I met Buddy in July of 2011 at the inaugural session of the University of Kentucky College of Education's Next Generation Leadership Academy. I had launched a new professional development curriculum that day; Buddy and associate superintendent, Thom Coffee, were there. The workshop I delivered exposed school leaders to the tenets of design thinking by having them empathetically interview secondary students and then, in an act of codesign, work shoulder to shoulder with those same students in the workshop to design an improved instructional experience for them. I argued that day (and still do) that when school leaders are able to empathize with those they serve, they can design an environment of surprise and delight. I further proposed that this is what great schools do. Something in that suggestion, and in the workshop with the students, sparked an idea between Buddy and Thom: we need to hear from our students.

Around that time 39 percent of students met state benchmarks for college and career readiness. There were two mobile devices in the district. No Advanced Placement or honors classes existed. Yes, Eminence is a small district, but Buddy and Thom embarked on a journey I've seen few, if any, district-level leaders take: they talked to every student in the district. They asked questions like "What is your idea of the perfect school?" and "What are things you like and don't like about your school?" What they learned was revelatory. Students yearned for authentic, hands-on learning; they wanted to be known by their teachers; they wanted to learn using modern technology. And while they didn't voice it explicitly, the time students were spending on tests was excessive. What Buddy and Thom developed was the Framework of Innovation for Reinventing Education or, as they like to say, Eminence became a school on F.I.R.E.

The F.I.R.E. approach developed at Eminence comprises five elements:

1. Anytime, anywhere learning, where all high school students are issued a MacBook Pro; instruction is offered in traditional, blended, and online formats; and the district's school bus is Wi-Fi equipped.

2. Personalized learning, where students have choice in their electives and personalized learning goals are set with students.
3. Comprehensive academic systems of support that allow for core classes, intervention, enrichments, and electives based on student need along with an advisor/advisee mentoring program.
4. Early college access through a partnership with Bellarmine University, offering seven credit hours of college courses per semester to juniors and seniors who meet ACT benchmarks. Students travel from Eminence to Bellarmine on the district's Wi-Fi-equipped bus.
5. Student voice, manifesting itself in a Student Voice Team that is an active participant in all district decision making.

Performance-based assessment via standards-based grading, project-based learning, and panel reviews for graduation of each school. In panel reviews, students in kindergarten and grades 5, 8, and 12 defend their learning in front of a panel of teachers and administrators. Students learn in a mastery environment that eschews test preparation completely.

The result? In 2016, Eminence was the first district in Kentucky to reach 100 percent on the benchmarks for college and career readiness for its graduates, up from 39 percent two years prior.[6] This, in spite of Thom Coffee's estimate that the district has reduced the time students spend on teaching to the test by 75 percent.

In addition, Eminence Independent School District codified surprise and delight into its district strategy. The policy reads as follows: "Woven throughout all we do is the concept of Surprise and Delight. We want each student, staff, and stakeholder to be continually amazed and engaged each and every day. We want to create and foster an environment where creativity and customer service abound in all aspects of our school. Whether great or small, the element of 'Surprise and Delight' is the essence of our organization."[7]

Leaders Failing Up

Garth Nichols is the vice principal of Student Engagement and Experiential Development at Havergal College, an independent K–12 girls school in Toronto, Canada. This is a story of how Garth didn't let fear of failure or fear of rejection diminish his spirit. This is how he embraced failing up.

At Havergal students may run for the elected office of prefect. To be a prefect within the school is to have a visible leadership role on campus. With a student body of just under a thousand and fifteen prefect slots, students who are elected prefect have a prominent role in the school. Prefects represent students within the school and represent the student body to parents and other stakeholders outside of the school. It's a sought-after role.

When a student is elected to the office of prefect, she is informed of what *portfolio*—there are twelve—she will oversee. There is an arts prefect, a sports prefect, a wellness prefect, a community prefect, a social council prefect, a student council prefect, and so on.

When students run for prefect, they may state which of the portfolios they are most interested in. A student might, say, express an interest in arts and wellness. Should she be elected she would, as one of her first duties, meet with Garth and key incoming and outgoing student leaders to be informed of her portfolio assignment.

Garth had just entered his third year as a school leader at Havergal. He was only now starting to get a hang of the culture, organizational system, and ways of working at the school. As the administrator overseeing the prefect system, he considered ideas that might make that system more effective and better serve the school. Garth had a hypothesis: What if instead of running for prefect, a student ran for the portfolio?

Garth first convened a group of teachers to converse, much as he had students and teachers do when developing the school's smartphone policy, and asked them to walk in others' shoes. They tackled questions such as, What do you think parents would say and feel about this idea? What do you think the students would say? What do you think other faculty would say and feel? What do you say? The feedback he received on his idea was polarized—there was no middle ground. Faculty said either "status quo please" or "this is a great idea."

Then Garth took his hunch to the students in the same manner. He presented the polarized findings from the faculty panel to the student council. The unanimous reaction of the students was "Bad idea. Keep the status quo."

Garth shelved the idea. But not before writing up the findings of the process so if the topic were to come up again, the school could go back and look at what was decided and how it was decided.

The big lesson here is this. Garth's work is an example of how a school leader uses steps from design thinking to put an interesting question (read: challenge, hunch, hypothesis) in front of the school community, talk through scenarios and user reactions, and then listen to the feedback to decide whether to go forward or to "murder your darlings."[8]

When Garth told me this story, he reflected on what he learned from the experience. He said, "I ask myself, 'What have I learned? What have I learned about how this school takes up change? What have I learned about the prefect election process itself? What have I learned about what the students see and value?' So, for me, it was a gift to be able to pull the curtain back a little more to better understand our students and my colleagues. I failed, but I learned."

Leaders who embrace the mind-sets associated with failing up (being flexible, being iterative, exhibiting creative confidence, and embracing ambiguity) are in a stronger position to pose an idea, provide a platform for collecting feedback on that idea, and in turn demonstrate respect, compassion, and empathy for what the community feels. Their ideas may not always work. Design thinking provides a process that gives school leaders permission to imagine what the future might look like and then empathetically, respectfully, and compassionately find out.

40+ WAYS TO GET TO KNOW YOUR STUDENTS

These ideas are offered in no particular order.

1. Set up home visits with your students.
2. Interview every student in the school.
3. Spend an entire day with a kid in the summer.
4. Invite some students to visit you at your house.
5. Video chat with students at night.
6. Trade lives for a day (teachers trade places with students).
7. Have students draw a picture of their morning.
8. If your students wear uniforms, wear the same uniform to school.
9. Ask students how things are going.
10. Notice how students take care of themselves.
11. Notice how students talk to each other.
12. Eat lunch with students.
13. Ask a student and his or her family out for a casual dinner.
14. Hold parent-teacher conferences at students' homes.
15. Take students to the movies.
16. Interact with students on social media.
17. Connect with students' families via Skype, Zoom, Google Hangouts, FaceTime, or other social media.

18. Offer homework help via Skype, Zoom, Google Hangouts, FaceTime, and so on.
19. Invite students to a board game night at your house.
20. Play online games with students.
21. Ask students to make a how-to video designed to show teachers how to play popular video games.
22. Play on a sports team with students and/or family members.
23. Form a community intramural team (e.g., a softball team) composed of teachers and students.
24. Create a start-of-the-year questionnaire.
25. Students and teachers walk in each other's shoes—literally:
    a. Select a location to conduct the activity, preferably a level walking surface, and mark off a distance of 200 meters (about 220 yards).
    b. Ask students to bring at least one spare pair of shoes to school (even extras if they have them) the day of the activity.
    c. Have students place the shoes at the starting line according to size.
    d. Students and teachers select a pair of shoes to wear that are not their own. The shoes must be any size other than their own and must belong to the opposite gender.
    e. Participants walk the assigned distance in someone else's shoes. They may not remove the shoes until they have completed the course.
26. Create a time to have a one-on-one coffee or lunch date with a student. Do this with each student in the school.
27. Hold a family fun gathering outside of school hours on school grounds such as family yoga night, or a book exchange, craft night, etc.
28. Let students teach a class.
29. Conduct team-building exercises for opening up student conversations, like trust walks and trust falls.
30. Walk the neighborhood of your school:
    a. Walk the various neighborhoods that your students live in to see where they come from.
    b. Notice how you feel as you travel through each neighborhood on foot.

    c. Ask yourself if this is how your students are sometimes feeling.

31. Play "What's in the Bag?" This lets all students relate to one another and gives you insight into who your students are.

    a. On the first day of school, give each student a brown bag.

    b. Explain to the students that they are to bring in three objects from home that represents a positive feeling about their home life. These can be pictures or photographs, but don't have to be as long as they are an object or an image.

    c. In class, students explain what their three objects are, why they chose them, and how the objects play into their home life.

    d. Give students the opportunity to share out loud with classmates; sit with the students when they share.

32. Interact with a student you don't know well. Write a couple sentences about who you think they are; then share and allow the student to refute your assumptions.

33. Allow students to share about themselves by bringing in a favorite food. Let the food item be a springboard for questions about why they like that particular food, how it makes them feel when they eat it, or what memories they may have about it (this works even if the food is not homemade).

34. Define empathy with students as a class.

35. Have students write preconceived notions of the teacher.

36. Have students create a time log of all their daily activities to see how they actually spend their time.

37. Hold a class discussion using Google Docs, AnswerGarden.ch, or GoSoapBox.com.

38. Give each student a composition book and ask them to journal once a day about who they are. Each week pick a theme that pertains to a personal connection for the student—one related, for example, to mom, dad, grandparents, siblings, neighbors, people of diversity in the community, and so on. Once a day, take time to share.

39. Plan a lunch bunch—invite students you see as struggling to a monthly lunch with your instructional team, grade-level team, or design team.

40. Invite family members to visit the classroom and share stories of their family history—for example, as first-, second-, third-, or fourth-generation Americans.

41. Have students create an "I am" ethnography video. Consider creating one yourself. Share the videos in an in-class film festival. Discuss the similarities and differences in everyone's lives.

42. Model self-disclosure through your own journals and videos.

43. Go to all the teachers of one student and do that kid's homework for that night.

44. Convene a monthly assembly inviting members of the interfaith community to talk about their faith and cultural traditions.

45. Eat in the lunch area with the kids.

46. Have students fill in the following: "When _____ happened, it changed my life." and share with the class.

47. Ride the school bus.

EMPATHETIC INTERVIEW EXERCISE:
WHAT WORKS? WHAT COULD BE IMPROVED?

This interview exercise is adapted from one I developed with my colleague Todd Hurst to support the professional development of school district design teams working to address education and workforce challenges in schools in southwest Indiana. Todd is the director of education and workforce at the Indiana nonprofit Regional Opportunity Initiatives and has been supporting the application of design thinking to address community challenges in the region for several years.

INSTRUCTIONS

Read the following interview transcript of an empathetic interview between a design team member and a school teacher. Jot down positive and negative aspects of the conversation. Note where the interviewer used best practices and where he made mistakes or missteps.

Now pair up with a partner. Share your notes with the person sitting next to you and talk about what you would do differently if you were leading this conversation. Together, fill out the plus/delta quadrant at the end of this exercise, making note of what parts of this conversation work well, what could be improved, what questions you have now, and what new ideas you may have for subsequent interviews.

If you are part of a larger group, after talking with your neighbor and completing the plus/delta quadrant, ask someone to lead a discussion with the entire group about what was discovered in this exercise.

INTERVIEW TRANSCRIPT

Design team member: Thank you for taking the time to talk with me today.

Teacher: Not a problem. Thanks for asking!

Design team member: Absolutely. So, I'm going to ask you a few questions about your experience here in the district. If you feel uncomfortable with any of my questions, you definitely don't have to answer. All of your responses will remain confidential. Before we begin, do you have any questions for me?

Teacher: I don't think so.

Design team member: Great. Then let's get started. So, my first question is, Can you tell me about your experience here at Bay Laurel Middle School?

Teacher: Like, as an employee?

Design team member: Sure . . .

Teacher: Okay, well, I came to the school five years ago after having taught at the high school for three years. Overall, I think the experience has been positive. I really like the other teachers here at the school and the kids are great. There are of course some frustrating aspects . . . technology integration has been difficult because we were just given computers and told to implement without any real guidance. But that's about it, I suppose.

Design team member: Yeah, the technology issue is something that has come up a lot. Other participants have indicated that the district launched a one-to-one laptop initiative to keep up with the district next door. Do you agree with that?

Teacher: Totally. We were losing kids to that district and I believe this is the district leadership's way of combating that.

Design team member: Okay. Thanks for sharing. What are some other frustrations you have had with the district?

(Design team member waits one second. Hearing no response, he continues.)

Design team member: I mean, I don't want to put words in your mouth, but maybe you have had a time when you felt as though the school leadership didn't hear what you had to say.

Teacher: I don't really think I have felt any frustrations like that. For the most part I'm pretty happy with everything.

Design team member: Okay, so on the other end, can you talk to me about what your hopes and dreams for the school district are?

Teacher: Well, I guess I hope that we have a meaningful educational experience that serves each and every student. I would love to see our students engaged with relevant, exciting curriculum that prepares them for a successful future.

Design team member: I'm really interested in your use of the word *successful* here. How would you define that word?

Teacher: I think it really comes down to being able to find gainful employment and contribute to society.

Design team member: Do you think that definition is common across the community or even your school?

Teacher: I don't know. It's not something I've ever asked anyone about. I think for much of our community success has been defined as getting a bachelor's degree, but I'm not convinced that's right for everyone.

Design team member: Right! I've been visiting a lot of employers recently and many have indicated their biggest difficulty is in filling jobs that require only a high school diploma . . . some of those jobs get paid more than I do with a master's degree!

Teacher: Isn't that crazy! Maybe I should look at some of those jobs?

Design team member: I know, right? Okay, so building upon our last question, do you have any other hopes for the community more broadly? Not just the school district.

Teacher: Hmm. I don't know. That's a tough question . . . I'll have to think about that for a minute.

Design team member: Okay. *(Design team member allows the silence and waits.)*

Teacher: Well, I guess I hope that our community becomes a place that people want to come to. I hope it becomes a place where people want to live. I feel like recently we have been slowly dying as a community.

Design team member: Can you elaborate on why you think that is happening?

Teacher: I suppose it's a lack of hope.

Design team member: Hmm . . . Okay. Well, unfortunately, that's all the time we have allotted for this interview. Thank you so much for agreeing to participate.

Teacher: Thank you.

Here are some pluses and deltas to consider about this interview. What else besides these did you notice?

Pluses

- The interviewer delved into the meaning of an otherwise common word in schools, *successful*, to find out what it meant to the teacher.
- The interviewer asked the teacher to elaborate on why she perceived their community is slowly dying.

Deltas

- The interviewer missed an opportunity to use the five whys when the teacher brought up her frustration about the integration of technology. In the follow-up question, the interviewer turned the exchange essentially into a yes/no response. The interviewer could have expanded this exchange and delved into likes/dislikes, feelings, and unmet needs.
- When asking the teacher if she has other frustrations, the interviewer waited only one second for a response and then started to put words in the teacher's mouth (after first saying he didn't want to do that). This took the teacher out of the role of being an expert of her own experience and in the position of affirming or denying she had experienced something the interviewer had lived through. The interviewer should have waited seven to ten seconds and then offered a neutral prompt like, "Even something that seems like a small frustration is okay to share."

Plus/Delta Quadrant for Capturing Feedback

- The interviewer didn't take up a rich opportunity to understand what the teacher meant by "lack of hope" in the community.

Discussion Questions

1. Where in the interview could the five whys technique have been used?
2. What are some ways to ask "why" repeatedly without sounding repetitive or annoying?
3. In what ways would an open-ended question like the following increase what you know about the life of the person you were interviewing: "If you were telling a new acquaintance about yourself, would you talk about being a teacher? What else would you say about yourself?"

NOTES

Preface

1. David Weinberger, *Too Big to Know: Rethinking Knowledge Now That the Facts Aren't the Facts, Experts Are Everywhere, and the Smartest Person in the Room Is the Room* (New York: Basic Books, 2011), xiii.

Introduction

1. Horst Rittel and Melvin Webber, "Dilemmas in a General Theory of Planning," *Policy Sciences* 4 (1973): 160.
2. Rittel and Webber, 160.
3. Jon Kolko, "Desgin Thinking Comes of Age," *Harvard Business Review* (September, 2015).
4. Ingo Rauth et al., "Design Thinking: An Educational Model Towards Creative Confidence" (paper presented at the 1st International Conference on Design Creativity, ICDC 2010, Kobe, Japan, November 29–December 1 2010).
5. Diefentahaler, Annette, Laura Moorhead, Sandy Speicher, Charla Bear, and Deirdre Cerminaro. "Thinking & Acting Like a Designer: How Design Thinking Supports Innovation in K-12 Education." World Innovation Summit for Education, September 2017. https://www.wise-qatar.org/2017 -wise-research-design-thinking
6. John Maeda, "Design in Tech Report 2017," https://desgnintech.report.
7. John Maeda, "Design in Tech Report 2016," https://desgnintech.report.
8. Maeda, 2016.
9. Kolko, "Desgin Thinking Comes of Age."
10. Richard Buchanan, "Wicked Problems in Design Thinking," *Design Issues* 8, no. 2 (1992); Donald A. Norman, *The Design of Everyday Things* (New York: Basic Books, 2002); Rittel and Webber, "Dilemmas in a General Theory of Planning"; and Herbert A. Simon, *The Sciences of the Artificial*, 3rd ed. (Cambridge, MA: MIT Press, 1996).

11. Maeda, "Design in Tech Report 2016."
12. Maeda, 2016.
13. Alfredo Costilla, "Empathic Design Guidelines in Healthcare for Successful Product Development" (Master of Design thesis, University of Cincinnati, 2011).
14. Costilla, 29.
15. Frederick Hess, *Cage-Busting Leadership* (Cambridge, MA: Harvard Education Press, 2013), xiii.
16. Richard Boland and Fred Collopy, eds., *Managing as Designing* (Stanford, CA: Stanford Business Books, 2004).
17. James L. Adams, *Conceptual Blockbusting: A Guide to Better Ideas*, 4th ed.(New York: Basic Books, 2001), 7.
18. Adams, 7.
19. Maeda, "Design in Tech Report 2016."
20. N. Bennett, C. Wise, and P. A. Woods, *Distributed Leadership* (Nottingham, England: National College of School Leadership, 2003), 3.
21. Phillip Hallinger, "The Evolving Role of American Principals: From Managerial to Instructional to Transformational Leaders," *Journal of Educational Administration* 30, no. 3 (1992).
22. Hallinger, 40.
23. Hallinger, 40.
24. Jesse Bacon has since been named superintendent of Bullitt County (KY) Public Schools.

Chapter 1

1. IDEO, *The Field Guide to Human-Centered Design: Design Kit* (San Francisco, CA: IDEO, 2015).
2. Frog, *Collective Action Toolkit* (San Francisco: Frog Design, 2012).
3. IDEO, *Design Thinking for Educators Toolkit* (San Francisco, CA: IDEO, 2012).
4. Jeanne Liedtka, Tim Ogilvie, and Rachel Brozenske, *The Designing for Growth Field Book: A Step-by-Step Project Guide* (New York: Columbia Business School Publishing, 2014).
5. Leslie Odom, *Failing Up: How to Take Risks, Aim Higher, and Never Stop Learning* (New York: Feiwel and Friends, 2018).
6. IDEO, *Design Thinking for Educators Toolkit*.
7. IDEO, *Toolkit*.
8. IDEO, *Toolkit*.

Chapter 2

1. IDEO, *Human Centered Design Field Guide*, 2nd ed. (San Francisco, CA: IDEO, 2011).
2. IDEO, *Design Thinking for Educators Toolkit* (San Francisco, CA: IDEO, 2012).

3. Warren Berger, *Glimmer: How Design Can Transform Your Life, and Maybe Even the World* (New York: Penguin Press, 2009), 27.

4. Hasso Plattner Institute of Design, *Bootcamp Bootleg* (Stanford, CA: Hasso Plattner Institute of Design, Stanford University, 2010). https://dschool .stanford.edu/resources/the-bootcamp-bootleg

5. Hasso Plattner, *Bootcamp.*

6. IDEO, *Human Centered Design Field Guide* 2nd ed. (San Francisco, CA: IDEO, 2011).

7. Hasso Plattner, *Bootcamp.*

8. IDEO, *Field Guide.*

Chapter 3

1. Dave Gray, "Updated Empathy Map Canvas," Medium, July 15, 2017, https://medium.com/the-xplane-collection/updated-empathy-map-canvas -46df22df3c8a.

2. Jill Thompson, "Building Empathy with Teachers,." Inside the Classroom, Outside the Box!, December 24 2018, https://insidetheclassroomoutside thebox.wordpress.com/2018/12/24/building-empathy.

3. Hasso Plattner Institutue of Design, *Bootcamp Bootleg* (Stanford, CA: Hasso Plattner Institute of Design, Stanford University, 2010).

Chapter 4

1. Brian Mullen, Craig Johnson, and Eduardo Salas, "Productivity Loss in Brainstorming Groups: A Meta-Analytic Integration," *Basic and Applied Social Psychology* 12, no. 1 (1991).

2. Tomas Chamorro-Premuzic, "Why Group Brainstorming Is a Waste of Time," *Harvard Business Review*, March 25, 2015.

3. Jeanne Liedtka and Tim Ogilvie, *Designing for Growth: A Design Thinking Tool Kit for Managers* (New York: Columbia University Press, 2011).

4. Hasso Plattner Institute of Design, *Bootcamp Bootleg* (Stanford, CA: Hasso Plattner Institute of Design, Stanford University, 2010); IDEO, *The Field Guide to Human-Centered Design* (Palo Alto, CA: IDEO, 2015).

5. Rikke Dam, "Define and Frame Your Design Challenge by Creating Your Point of View and Ask 'How Might We,'" Interaction Design Foundation, www.interaction-design.org/literature/article/define-and-frame-your -design-challenge-by-creating-your-point-of-view-and-ask-how-might -we.

6. Hasso Plattner Institute of Design.

7. Catlin Tucker, "Borrowing a Powerful Brainstorm Protocol from IDEO," https://catlintucker.com/2017/09/brainstorms.

8. Tucker; Liedtka and Ogilvie.

9. Dave Gray, "The Anti-Problem," Gamestorming, October 27, 2010, http:// gamestorming.com/the-anti-problem.

10. Chauncey Wilson, "Using Brainwriting for Rapid Idea Generation," *Smashing Magazine*, December 13, 2013.

11. Link MV, "6-3-5 Method (Brainwriting)," www.youtube.com/watch?v=TR 1i1PPd8ZU.

12. Hasso Plattner Institute of Design.

13. Corey Wainwright, "12 Brainstorming Techniques for Unearthing Better Ideas from Your Team," Hubspot, July 16, 2018, https://blog.hubspot.com /marketing/team-brainstorm-ideas.

14. Wainwright.

15. Wainwright.

16. Karen Leggett Dugosh, Paul B. Paulus, Evelyn J. Roland, and Huei-Chuan Yang, "Cognitive Stimulation in Brainstorming," *Journal of Personality and Social Psychology* 79, no. 5 (2000): 722–35.

Chapter 5

1. IDEO, *From Ideas to Action Toolkit* (San Francisco, CA: IDEO, 2015).

2. Pixar Studios, "Story Spine: Activity One," Khan Academy, www.khan academy.org/partner-content/pixar/storytelling/story-structure/a/activity -1-struc.

3. "Storyboard That" Digital Storytelling, www.storyboardthat.com; "Scenes," https://experience.sap.com/designservices/approach/scenes.

4. Dan Ryder, Wicked Focus, www.wickedfocus.com.

Chapter 6

1. Jeanne Liedtka, Tim Ogilvie, and Rachel Brozenske, *The Designing for Growth Field Book: A Step-by-Step Project Guide* (New York: Columbia Business School Publishing, 2014).

2. IDEO, *Human-Centered Design Toolkit*, 2nd ed. (Palo Alto, CA: IDEO, 2011).

3. Matt Pearsall, "The Challenge of Advisory and Why It's Worth the Effort," *ALME Magazine*, October 2017.

4. Carol Weiss, "Nothing as Practical as Good Theory: Exploring Theory-Based Evaluation for Comprehensive Community Initiatives for Children and Families," in *New Approaches to Evaluating Community Initiatives: Concepts, Methods, and Contexts*, ed. James Connell et al. (Washington, DC: Aspen Institute, 1995).

5. Ellen Taylor-Powell and Ellen Henert, *Developing a Logic Model: Teaching and Training Guide* (Madison, WI: University of Wisconsin-Extension, 2008).

6. Amy Schade, *Pilot Testing: Getting It Right (Before) the First Time* (Fremont, CA: Nielsen Norman Group, 2015).

7. Miles Woken, "Advantages of a Pilot Study: Planning Research Papers 7" (Springfield, IL: Center for Teaching and Learning).

8. Taylor-Powell and Henert.
9. Rural Health Information Hub, *Common Implementation Challenges* (Grand Forks, ND: Rural Health Information Hub, 2019).

Chapter 7

1. William Easterly, *The White Man's Burden: Why the West's Efforts to Aid the Rest Have Done So Much Ill and So Little Good* (New York: Penguin, 2007, 5.
2. Easterly, 5.
3. Lisa Morehouse, "Teaching with Passion: Advice for Young Educators," Edutopia, March 25, 2008, www.edutopia.org/jonathan-kozol-advice -teachers.
4. Claudia Dixon, "Teacher Leaders and Students Co-designing Learning," September 22, 2016, www.youtube.com/watch?v=2j0iiEtQk-U.
5. Kentucky General Assembly, www.lrc.ky.gov/lrcpubs/rr382.pdf.
6. "Improving Assessment Through School on FIRE—Eminence Independent Schools, Kentucky," *Progress* (blog), U.S. Department of Education, December 5, 2016, https://sites.ed.gov/progress/2016/12/improving -assessment-through-school-on-fire-eminence-independent-schools -kentucky.
7. Eminence Independent Schools, School on F.I.R.E., www.eminence.k12 .ky.us/docs/School%20on%20Fire%20Framework.pdf.
8. Arthur Quiller-Couch, *On the Art of Writing: Lectures Delivered in the University of Cambridge, 1913–1914, by Sir Arthur Quiller-Couch* (Cambridge, England: Cambridge University Press, 1916 / Pinnacle Press, 2017).

ACKNOWLEDGMENTS

I'm eternally grateful to my partner, Beth Rous, who was unfailingly compassionate regarding this project. She was reader, critic, editor, counsel, cheerleader, and imposter-syndrome buster. Thank you for your love and support.

To my daughters, Chelsea, Olivia, Abigail, and Mackenzie, who during their childhoods allowed me to call anything that didn't go quite right "a prototype." You all, however, are not prototypes—each of you came out just right the first time. I love you very much.

To the individuals I had the opportunity to work with and be mentored by at the Stanford Learning Lab (SLL), this book wouldn't exist if I hadn't met you. To Larry Leifer, Sheri Shepherd, and Larry Friedlander, thank you for a rich, interdisciplinary ride. I especially want to thank my teammates in the research and assessment group at SLL, aka the A-Team, Carolyn Ybarra, Helen Chen, Evonne Schaeffer (you are missed, Evonne), Sigrid Mueller, and Francis Montell. Thank you for being part of an amazing, challenging, and rewarding experience. And to Melissa Regan, Charles Kerns, Reinhold Steinbeck, George Toye, Bob Smith, Ade Mabogunje, Gina Funaro, and Harrianne Mills. My view of the world became broader and more optimistic because of each of you.

You might not think that interactions over a couple of weeks could change you forever. But that was the case for me when I got to know Bernie Roth, Doug Wilde, and the late Rolf Faste during their Creativity Workshop for Professors at Stanford. Bernie taught me there's no such thing as have to, only want to. Doug taught me that diverse teams outperform homogeneous teams every time. And Rolf never let me forget how important it is to exercise your brain. I'm grateful you've all remained in a corner of my mind because you each made me a better teacher, designer, and person.

I first worked with Dan Gilbert at the Stanford Center for Innovations in Learning (SCIL), and coincidentally we both left Silicon Valley for the middle of the country within a year of each other. We both discovered that innovation in this country is not bound to the coasts. In Nebraska, Iowa, and Kentucky we found that the ideas in the Heartland can compete anywhere. Dan and I still collaborate to this day. You stimulate my thinking and keep me reaching, Dan. Thank you.

When Gunnar Backman and Tomas Erlandsson and I had coffee in the Cantor Arts Center's Rodin Sculpture Garden at Stanford one day, I didn't know we'd conclude the meeting by starting a company in Stockholm, Sweden. But that's what we did. Both of you have taught me so much. Through ups and downs and pivots we've become lifelong friends. Thanks for trusting me to take Open Eye into the start of its third decade.

Stig Hagström was not only a mentor and colleague at Stanford, a gracious neighbor in Menlo Park, and trusting friend but also a steadfast supporter of whatever I was doing. I miss you, Stig.

To Scott McCleod, Mary John O'Hair, Justin Bathon, Jayson Richardson, Wayne Lewis, Lars Björk, Tricia Browne-Ferrigno, Lu Young, and Carmen Coleman. You have supported my desire to craft a research and development agenda around design thinking. Thank you for your trust, collaboration, and friendship.

To Linda France and Eve Proffitt. Without you we would not have piloted the design thinking curriculum that has become a staple of the Next Generation Leadership Academy for nearly a decade, nor would we have prototyped what became the first design thinking course at the University of Kentucky.

The Next Generation Leadership Academy inspired folks like Buddy Berry and Thom Coffee to take the tenets of design thinking and go above and beyond what anyone considered possible in Eminence, Kentucky. Thank you, Buddy and Thom, for what you've done as educators to demonstrate the power of empathy and student agency.

To Nancy Walser, my editor at Harvard Education Press. Once upon a time a polite inquiry about my work appeared in my inbox. It was from Nancy and it started a conversation that later became this book. Nancy, you are unfailingly pleasant, persistent, and professional. Thank you for guiding me on this journey.

ABOUT THE AUTHOR

John B. Nash is an associate professor of educational leadership at the University of Kentucky, where he specializes in the design and prototyping of innovations in education and teaches a range of courses on design thinking, school technology leadership, and school reform. He is also the founding director of the Laboratory on Design Thinking in Education (dLab), an initiative within the University of Kentucky's College of Education. Nash is a former associate director for evaluation at the Stanford Center for Innovations in Learning and former associate director of assessment and research at the Stanford Learning Laboratory.

INDEX